THE MAKING OF A BLACK PSYCHOLOGIST

Dr. Earl Bracy

The Making Of A Black Psychologist
Copyright © 2020 **Dr. Earl Bracy**

All rights reserved. No part of this book may be used or reproduced by any means, graphic, electronic, or mechanical, including photocopying, recording, taping or by information storage and retrieval system without the written permission of the author except in the case of brief quotations embodied in critical articles and reviews.

Stratton Press Publishing
831 N Tatnall Street Suite M #188,
Wilmington, DE 19801
www.stratton-press.com
1-888-323-7009

Because of the dynamic nature of the Internet, any web addresses or links contained in this book may have changed since publication and may no longer be valid. The views expressed in the work are solely those of the author and do not necessarily reflect the views of the publisher, and the publisher hereby disclaims any responsibility for them.

ISBN (Paperback): 978-1-64895-157-2
ISBN (Hardback): 978-1-64895-274-6
ISBN (Ebook): 978-1-64895-158-9

Printed in the United States of America

I would like to dedicate this book to two people who meant the world to me. It saddened me deeply to lose them both, but their passing gave me a new insight into the true meaning of life.

I dedicate this book to my father, Reverend Gayle Bracy, a man who had an unending faith in God and who taught me how to live my life. Being a black man in the Deep South, he experienced a great deal of racism: discrimination, oppression, and racial hatred. In spite of being humiliated daily, he stood erect. Through this book, I hope that America and the world will better understand his life and the life of black men in general. As Jesus said to his Father while on the cross, "It is finished." And now I am saying to my father, in different terms, "Father, it is finished."

I also dedicate this book to my daughter, Yolanda Bracy, who had so much potential. Because of her untimely death, she was unable to tell her own story, but through my writings, she will. Tragic as it was, her death helped me to heighten my compassion and concern for those in grieving. Her presence continues to be around me in many ways, and she is smiling at the completion of a book that she remembers being only in the talking stages. I am sure she is asking, "What are you going to do next?"

ACKNOWLEDGMENT

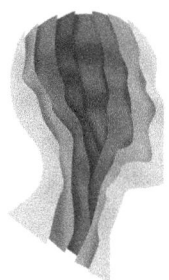

I would like to first thank God for providing me with good health, a sound mind, and directing my thoughts and my path in bringing this book to fruition. Secondly, I would like to thank my daughter and her husband, Sonia and Kevin Sledge, for collecting the needed pictures that depict my birthplace.

I would also like to thank my mother for being the loving mother that she is. Her strength, endurance, and resiliency were passed on to me and my siblings, and for that I am forever grateful.

I am much appreciative to Ms. Virginia Long, a great friend who spent many hours typing, revising, and editing this text. She knows my life story, and I've felt quite comfortable discussing it with her.

My thanks also go out to Ms. Tyesha Alexander, a great friend and colleague for encouraging me to bring this book to completion.

I also give thanks to a longtime friend Ms. Wanda Frazier, who helped clerically during the early stages of this book.

To my niece Lewkita Voit, who scanned, organized, and transferred all of the pictures to a disc, I give many thanks.

I am also appreciative to my niece Jacinda Bracy for discovering archival pictures that were critical in bringing this book together.

I give thanks to Father Fred Alexander, OCD, pastor of St. Mary's of the Hill Parish of Holy Hill, Wisconsin, for giving me space at Holy Hill to reflect, meditate, and write.

Many thanks go out to Father Carl Diederichs, pastor of All Saints Catholic Church in Milwaukee, Wisconsin, for his support, encouragement, and his awesome prayers.

I thank my sister, Mrs. Hannah Smith, for the work she did in retrieving the first names of my elementary and high school teachers and for filling in some of the gaps during my childhood.

Thanks also go out to my brothers, Harold Bracy and Lionell Bracy, and my sister, Mrs. Linda Bosby, for filling in the childhood gaps as well.

A SPECIAL TRIBUTE

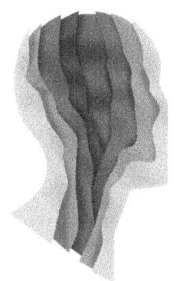

I would like to pay a special tribute to all of the teachers who taught me and others in elementary school at the all-black Anna T. Jeanes School in Fairhope, Alabama:

Mrs. Ida Holt
Mrs. Sally O'Cain
Mrs. Ida Boykin
Mr. Alvin Boykin (principal)
Ms. Anniece Hale
Ms. Bernice Hale
Mrs. Alice Bryant
Mrs. Willie Carter
Mrs. Irene Washington
Mr. Jeffery Washington
Mrs. Grace Nye
Mrs. Anna Bosby
Mrs. Marie Williams
Mrs. Lillian Valrie
Mrs. Helen Hamilton
Mrs. Vera Denton

I would also like to pay a special tribute to all of my high school teachers who taught at Baldwin County Training School in Daphne, Alabama:

Mr. Walker J. Carroll (principal)
Mrs. Thelma Carroll
Mr. Lemuel Taylor (vice principal)
Mrs. S. Taylor
Mr. Tommie Valrie
Mr. John Leonard
Mr. S. Hall
Mr. James Chancley
Mr. Thomas Lee
Mrs. Barbara Lee
Mr. John Montgomery
Mrs. Eleanor Harpe
Mr. Baily Yelding
Mr. Raymond Barnes

There were other teachers in elementary and high school who did not teach me but were a part of my overall development, and they are included in this tribute. All of these teachers cared deeply about all of the students, and in spite of racial oppression, they prepared us for a world that they knew would accept us only as second-class citizens, but they all stood erect and persevered in the face of bigotry. Even though they had college degrees, they were locked out of many institutions and mainstream society because of the color of their skin. Many of them have passed on, but their spirits are alive, and they need to know that their labor in the vineyard was not in vain. Those teachers who are still alive need to know that this former student recognized their commitment, their sacrifices, their struggles, their pain, and their hurt as well as their strength and perseverance. You prepared all of your students for life. To all of you, I appreciate your strength, knowledge, wisdom, resiliency, and determination. I would like to say again, thank you! Thank you! Thank you!

When I graduated from high school, our principal, Mr. Walker J. Carroll, said to me, "One day we will hear from you." He said this with a big smile on his face, and now I know what he meant.

CONTENTS

Acknowledgment 5

A Special Tribute 7

Chapter One: My Childhood Years in Rural Alabama
(Jim Crow Revisited)..13

Chapter Two: Living in Oak Creek, Wisconsin
(A Culture Shock) 53

Chapter Three: High School Years in the Segregated South 62

Chapter Four: My Northern Migration to Milwaukee...................92

Chapter Five: My Army Experience during the Vietnam War.....108

Chapter Six: Return to Milwaukee during the
"Me Generation" 119

Chapter Seven: My Personal Grief (The Untimely
Death of My Daughter)..169

Chapter Eight: My Personal Grief (My Father's Death) 185

Chapter Nine: A Loving Mother 197

About the Author..203

CHAPTER ONE

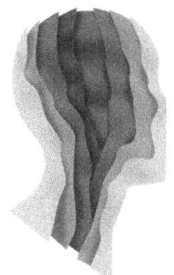

My Childhood Years in Rural Alabama (Jim Crow Revisited)

This book is being written to enlighten the minds of all those who read it. It is also being written to strengthen the hearts and minds of all those facing obstacles and adversities. There is nothing in this book that is untrue, and it is written as my profound contribution to humanity. I have asked God to guide my mind and my heart as I've prepared to go back in time and take a journey that has had many obstacles and roadblocks, before reaching the pinnacle of success as a black clinical psychologist.

I was born in Fairhope, Alabama, which is a small town on the eastern shore of the Mobile Bay. Fairhope has grown over the years because many people retire to this area. The population as of 2010 is approximately thirty thousand people.

Fairhope was founded in 1894, and the founders named their town Fairhope before it existed because they felt that it had a "fair hope of success." Since Fairhope sits right on the Mobile Bay, and the bay being a tributary of the Gulf of Mexico, one can see how the slave trade flourished in this area. Because Mobile was a port city, slave ships dropped off human cargo (slaves) in the port city of Mobile quite frequently. More than ten million black slaves were brought from the continent of Africa to the Southern United States and an equal amount or more died en route.

Fairhope is approximately twenty-two miles from Mobile, and this region is known for hot weather, thunderstorms, and hurricanes. As a young boy, I remember everyone boarding up their homes and businesses during the hurricane season. Due to my naivete, I did not understand the fierceness and devastation of a hurricane. I found it to be exciting, listening to the howling of the winds late at night, when the force of the hurricane was approaching. Due to the high winds, power lines were down, and we had no electricity. Sometimes the electricity was out for several days. Even in darkness, there was something exciting about not knowing what was going to happen from moment to moment. By my father being a minister, this gave me comfort and solace in knowing that his prayers would be answered and we'd be protected.

My mother has reminded me on many occasions that I was her toughest and most difficult delivery. I was delivered at home by a midwife, and on that night of September 13, when I was born, there was a fierce storm that was probably of hurricane proportion. Through the grace of God, my mother recuperated after giving birth to me. She still reminds me that I was the one who almost took her out of this world. My mother gave birth to twelve children (six boys and six girls), and I was the fourth oldest. Whenever I tell anyone how many siblings I have, they become in shock and in awe. It is also necessary to point out that for black families, this was a common phenomenon in the Deep South during that era.

In many instances, there existed what could be called a modern era of share cropping, and due to Jim Crow rules in the South, black families benefited because large families meant that everyone could work and this supplemented the family's income. My mother was a housewife, and she played the piano and organ at the church that my father copastored and at times pastored. My mother never took music lessons but could play almost any song. At the age of eighty-six, she still plays the piano for one or two churches.

Most of the black men in those days were common laborers, and the women were domestic housewives or they worked as servants and maids in the homes of white people. Even though segregation and separatism were the order of the day, there were many nice white people who were very generous and giving, who had good hearts, and who looked after the black families who worked for them, but they also went along with the status quo of segregation and "separate and unequal" facilities. We were not allowed to attend schools with white children, but there were many occasions when we had the opportunity to play and interact with them while working with my father. I remember my father trimming branches from several pine trees for a white family who had a large beautiful red brick ranch-style home with an enclosed back porch. I remember playing with the white kids of this family while my father worked on their property. He would often take my brothers and me with him on the many jobs he would get taking care of lawns, excavating and trimming trees. I particularly remember the white kids that we played with because the family did not seem prejudiced at all.

While on the back porch of their home, I remember watching *The Little Rascals*, cartoons and having lunch with them. What stands out in my mind more than anything else is the news flash that came on the television. It stated as follows: "President Eisenhower orders federal troops into Little Rock, Arkansas. Nine black students were attempting to integrate Little Rock High School, and federal troops were called in to protect them." It was ironic that during those turbulent and perilous times, we were breaking bread together and playing with little white kids in the seat of segregation, the Heart of Dixie. Interestingly, this area of the South rivaled South Africa in racial bigotry.

There were also many beautiful mansions along the Mobile Bay, often owned by white northerners who would spend the winter months in their homes along the bay.

Many of the homes were built with an antebellum look to them, and inside them were five or six bathrooms, three or four dining rooms, and more than one living room. I remember exploring the homes on many occasions and wishing one day that I could be so fortunate. The owners of these homes trusted my father, and when they returned to the northern states, they would leave the keys to their homes with him. While helping my father take care of the lawns and remove broken oak and pine limbs, we also fished, crabbed, and swam in Mobile Bay.

Our day would start at 6:00 a.m., and we often finished as the sun was going down. My brothers and I would use shrimp, earthworms, and salt pork for fishing bait. Whenever we caught a catfish, we would throw it back or use it for crab bait. The catfish was viewed as a scavenger fish, and today, it is viewed as a delicacy.

Several times during the year and especially during the summer and fall, Mobile Bay would give up a multitude of its fish, crabs, and shrimp when many of these creatures would come to shore in a dazed and confused state. Whenever this happened, everyone along Mobile Bay would call it a jubilee. Today, it is still called a jubilee. During the period of a jubilee, blacks and whites would bring out their sacks, nets, spears, and buckets to harvest a bountiful catch of dazed fish, crabs, and shrimp. As a young boy, I remember the grown-ups saying that the fish became ill because fresh water mixed with salt water. This notion still holds true today. Now that I am an adult, I still cannot help but wonder exactly what caused the fish to become ill and if eating them was okay.

Many black people had no place to keep the fish after they scooped them up from shore, so they would put them in a big tub with ice and salt them down after the fish had been eviscerated. When the fish were fried, you could definitely tell that they had been salted. This type of salt usage and salt preservation may also have something to do with the high hypertensive rates in blacks. One of the black men who was a pillar in the community used to deliver blocks of ice to people who had what was called an ice box, not a refrigerator. If I remember correctly, that block of ice would last for at least a week. I would guess that it weighed between sixty to seventy-five pounds. Another thing that stands out about Mobile Bay were the signs posted all along the bay that read, Whites Only. The families for whom my father worked did not post such signs. Even though my brothers, sisters, and I could swim in the bay, we were careful not to venture into the Whites Only areas.

Because of racism and discrimination, most black men and women held menial and low-paying jobs. When I started first grade, I remember two black male teachers in Fairhope. The most honorable profession was a teacher. The other profession where men wore a suit and tie was that of an insurance salesman. Black insurance salesmen worked for a black insurance company and sold life insurance policies to black people only. The other professions included chauffeurs, maître d's, common laborers, cooks, truck drivers, farm workers, and other jobs that required very little education.

When I was in elementary school, several of my classmates would bring a pocketful of change to school, and it was years later that I realized that they were getting the change from their fathers who were getting tips from being limousine drivers and maître d's at the Grand Hotel, which is now the Marriott, located in Point Clear, Alabama, on Mobile Bay.

Because of deep-seated racism and discrimination, the city of Fairhope had no black doctors, lawyers, engineers, accountants, or other professionals other than teachers. Even if qualified, when blacks came in, they were not hired in any capacity. I remember when the city of Fairhope hired its first black policeman, and he was not a high school graduate. He wore a uniform and carried a gun but could only arrest black people. It is also important to note that the city of Fairhope separated itself from the black section of Fairhope.

As a young boy, I remember streetlights in the white section of town, but the streetlights ran out in the black section of town. Also, the streets were paved in the white section of town, but the pavement stopped in the black section of town. Whenever there was a hard rain, the roads would become exceptionally muddy, and cars would often become stuck in the mud. Periodically, a bulldozer would come through and smooth out the roads after a hard rain. The driver of the bulldozer (a white man) would always wave to us and smile at us. As curious children, we would run and walk behind the bulldozer as he cleared the road. There was also something exciting about the bulldozer unearthing the fresh red dirt, and it was exciting to feel the coldness of the red clay. As young boys, it was fashionable to construct wooden wagons and go-carts and race each other on the freshly plowed dirt roads.

The state of Alabama also allowed its black prisoners to work on the roads, and they were responsible for cutting the grass and weeds along the highway in our neighborhoods and all over the county. There were also one or two prison guards who stood watch over them with a loaded rifle. It was a scene that we became accustomed to seeing. Interestingly, some of the prisoners were from the area. As a small boy, I remember the prisoners flirting with the black girls, and the white guards would not say anything as long as the prisoners (convicts) stayed in line.

Even though the grass and weeds were cut periodically, we received inadequate services in the black community. There was no such thing as having our garbage picked up by the city, but it was picked up for the white residents. Also, in the white neighborhood, the roads were paved, but we had to contend with dirt roads in the black community. Whenever it rained, the roads were extremely muddy and slippery.

The main highway coming out of the town of Fairhope was called Section Street, and when my father first moved to Fairhope, he was responsible for cutting down all of the trees and removing tree trunks and debris to open Section Street to the black community. Today, Section Street is a paved highway and a busy thoroughfare. Much progress has been made, and any black resident can have a light installed simply by requesting it. Door-to-door garbage service is also available today.

As a teenager growing up in Fairhope, Alabama, I can still remember being stopped by white police officers who would simply stop all black people to see if they had a valid driver's license. It is also interesting that this seemed to have coincided with the civil rights activities that were going on in Selma, Alabama, and other parts of the South. I witnessed on many occasions, many black people being stopped by white policemen for no reason other than to check a driver's license, and white residents were allowed to go through the "dragnet" without being stopped.

During this same era, which was the middle of the late 1960s, it was a common sight to see white men all over the county (Baldwin County, Alabama) driving pickup trucks with a rifle hanging from a rifle rack in the rear window. Many of them, who were regular civilians, also mounted red police lights in either their front dashboard or the rear window of their cars. There was an atmosphere of fear and uncertainty on the part of white citizens, especially men. They did not retaliate physically toward black people, but they were poised for the possibility of civil unrest like the riots that were spreading across northern cities. Many of these white men were calling themselves volunteer firefighters, and even as a teenager, I could see through the camouflage.

When I was a little boy, I was an avid reader, and one magazine, in particular, that I liked reading was *Jet* magazine, which is a black magazine that has been in existence for several decades. I remember reading about Emmit Till, a young black boy in Mississippi, who was killed and thrown in the Mississippi River for supposedly whistling at a white woman. I remember being fearful and suspicious of white males, and to this day, I find myself still having a mistrust of white males who have a southern accent.

Many years after Emmit Till was killed at the hands of southern racists, his mother stated that in spite of the disfigurement of his face, she chose to have a funeral with an open casket because she wanted the world to see the ugly face of racism.

As a young boy, growing up in Alabama, I remember my black elders in the community cautioning me and other young black males about whistling at white girls. It was an unwritten law that there was absolutely no flirting with white girls. There was a fear that if any flirtation occurred, you could be castrated or hanged by white men. It was common for black males to walk around holding their genitals, and I often wondered if this was done on an unconscious level, arriving from a fear of castration.

From about the age of five, I can remember working with my father on many jobs. Before I became a teenager, I worked in Irish potato fields. One of the black boys picking potatoes with us one day whistled at the white farmer's daughter, and she told her father who was our boss.

During this hot summer day, the temperature in the potato field was around ninety to ninety-five degrees, but the hot temperatures did not stop us from working all day. We did not know what was going on, but it was later told to us that the white farmer who had hundreds of acres of potatoes to be harvested was inches away from killing the black youth who whistled at his daughter.

According to the black man who transported us to the potato field daily and who was hired by the white farmer, the farmer's wife begged and pleaded with the farmer to spare the black youth's life, and luckily he did. During this era, there was an unwritten rule that blacks were seen as subservient, unequal, and oftentimes invisible.

From about the age of seven to twelve, I picked Irish potatoes every summer. As a matter of fact, all of my brothers and sisters who were old enough were awakened at 4:30 a.m. to work in the potato fields. Our day ended when it became dark, which was about 8:30 to 9:00 p.m.

There were many nights when we didn't get home until 11:00 p.m., due to the trucks being stuck at the potato shed because of a backup, usually due to a machinery malfunction. Other times, the truck drivers would spill a load of potatoes en route to the potato shed, and sometimes the driver would have to wait his turn to unload. It was not uncommon for the driver to be number 14 or so in line for unloading, and his truck was the truck that transported us home at night. The potatoes were picked by hand and put in potato sacks, and the sacks usually weighed between seventy-five to one hundred pounds full. As the potatoes were picked and sacked, the sacks were lined up in rows, and the truck driver would idle the truck so that it would move at a snail's pace while the strong black men and boys would load the sacks onto the truck. The sacks had to be stacked in such a way so that the pile was neat, and it was important for the pile to be sturdy to ensure a smooth transport to the potato shed.

When the potatoes were plowed by the white farmers, plowing into the dry earth produced a tremendous amount of dust. As I think back on those days, we must have been a sight for sore eyes. Our clothes were dusty, and our bodies were completely dusty. Most of the kids wore no shoes, so one can only imagine what our feet looked like after being in ninety-degree heat and dust all day. The white farmer would shut the plows down at noon every day for lunch.

During the lunch hour, we were loaded onto a big truck and usually taken to a general store where we bought things like cinnamon rolls, bread for making sandwiches, luncheon meat, bologna, orange drinks, and sodas. My father would also roast peanuts in the shell the night before, and I would help him bag them and sell them the next day. The selling price was usually a nickel a bag. We usually did not have money to buy lunch, so the white farmer would advance the black man in charge money to dispense for lunch, and it was taken from our pay at the end of the week. We were paid three to five cents for every bushel of potatoes we picked, and on a good day, I could pick approximately three hundred bushels.

In the middle of the potato field, there was a big wooden barrel with a spigot, full of ice water. The barrel sat inside of what we called a croker sack, and the sack was filled with ice. The adults made sure that salt was poured on the ice to prevent it from melting too fast.

As kids we were always happy when the tractor used for plowing potatoes broke down because this gave us time to play, although we were not making any money. As young boys, we loved sports, and we always found ways to improvise. We would pick the biggest potato and use it as a football and would actually play football in the middle of the potato field. We had very good receivers, including myself.

Sometimes during a lull in activity, I remember lying on my back in the middle of the potato field and looking up at the sky and wondering about the universe and what my life would be like as an adult.

I remember one day, while picking potatoes, I may have suffered a heat stroke. At that time, I was probably around ten years of age. The temperature was between ninety-two to ninety-seven degrees, but the rising temperatures never stopped us from working. During this strange illness, I experienced chills, fever, stomach cramps, a headache, dehydration, vomiting, and transient blindness from looking directly into the sun. The women who came to the potato fields usually wore long dresses, a scarf, and a hat to protect their hair from the dust. The older women, especially, were deeply religious, and during those days,

I remember them singing Negro spirituals as they worked. One lady, in particular, nursed me back to health.

During this episode of illness, I felt extremely weak and could hardly move. This very religious lady, who I saw as an angel, laid me on a pile of croker sacks and patted my face and forehead down with an ice-cold towel. I remember her saying, "He's burning up," and she must have been referring to my fever. She also made sure that I was under a shade tree, where she cradled me in her arms and gave me small sips of 7-Up. I remember her putting her hand on my forehead and praying for me, and I truly believe that she may have saved my life. As a child, I never told my mother about this ordeal, but I did tell her when I became an adult, and she was shocked and appalled that I never told her what had happened.

My father also contracted his services to harvest Irish potatoes, and he was known and respected by many of the white farmers. He was paid a flat fee for bringing in crews to harvest the potatoes. It was also common for my father to bring all of my siblings to the potato field, and together we could yield anywhere from 1,200 to 1,500 bushels per day, which yielded $36 to $45 per day as a family.

My mother stayed home and always had a big meal prepared when we came home. I never remember her coming to the potato field, although she informed me years later that she did, but she couldn't stand the hot sun.

While picking potatoes, we always ran into obstacles. It was not uncommon to run into ant beds and snakes. I don't remember anyone being bitten by a snake, but we walked into many ant beds. I remember being stung particularly between my fingers and toes on multiple occasions. The women were quick to mother us whenever we were stung. They always had a bottle of rubbing alcohol available. It was always frightening for us whenever we saw a snake severed by the farmer's plow as he was unearthing the potatoes. Even though the snake was cut in half and sometimes in quarters, it was still moving vigorously as if it was going to continue to live. Many of the elders would tell us that the snake would continue to live and regenerate. As kids, we believed the stories that the elders would tell us. Whenever we started our day by seeing a snake entrapped in the farmer's plow, we had a great deal of anxiety about being confronted by another snake. To this day, I still have a fear of snakes.

While picking potatoes, one could end up with multiple abrasions to your fingers and particularly your nail bed. Interestingly enough, black people were not the only people who picked potatoes. Truckloads of Mexicans (men, women, and children) came from Texas to Alabama to harvest potatoes and other crops. Even though we worked side by side, there was a physical and emotional distance kept between us. This may have been by design on the part of the white farmers to prevent unity or the men may have planned it on an unconscious level to prevent interracial mingling between the males and females. Another reason that there was no mingling was because of the language barrier. The Mexicans spoke Spanish and may not have understood very much English. As a small boy, I saw Mexican girls and women as being extremely beautiful and attractive.

As far as picking potatoes, the Mexicans had a different technique. We picked our potatoes in bushel baskets and poured them in croker sacks while the Mexicans hooked a sack between their legs and put the potatoes directly into the sack. This technique was also a lot faster. The Mexicans were also nomadic in that they traveled from state to state harvesting crops that were in season. They often moved into an abandoned house without electricity or running water. As far as I could tell, the electricity was never turned on, and they would always burn candles at night. There were also as many as thirty people living in one house. On weekends, the Mexican women stayed home and washed, and I'm not exactly sure where the men were, but I always got a sense that they were out drinking. As a little boy, I was very observant.

Sometimes the Irish potato season coincided with the watermelon season, and oftentimes, a farmer would grow multiple crops. If a potato farmer would grow watermelons as well, we would sometimes wander over to his watermelon field if the tractor used for plowing potatoes broke down. We would literally bust open the watermelon and eat the most center core, the "heart." We were also stung by bees on multiple occasions. The bees were attracted to the sweetness of the melons, and they became our most formidable foe.

Sometimes the white farmer would find out that we had invaded his melon patch, and the black man who contracted to harvest his crops would reprimand us. My father also harvested watermelons, and we worked for other black contractors as well. The watermelons would be loaded onto trucks, and we would usually stack them as high as they would go.

As energetic and adventurous boys, we enjoyed sitting on top of the watermelons as the truck roared down the highway. There was something exciting about almost having to sit on the cab of a truck that was loaded with watermelons. We felt like hunters who had captured a prize, and we loved the attention that people gave us as we sat proudly on top of our catch.

When picking or harvesting watermelons, one had to be in top physical condition. This was a tedious job, which entailed three to five guys lined up on each side of the truck as it slowly moved through the watermelon patch. Temperatures ranged from eighty-eight to ninety-five degrees. The melons had to be cut from the vine and lined up in rows. They then had to be thrown from person to person until the melon reached the last person closest to the truck. That person then tossed the melon to one of two guys who loaded the truck from the front to the rear. This took some finesse because the melons had to be placed in such a way that they did not fall.

The driver of the truck kept a steady pace of about three miles per hour, and if the truck stopped abruptly, the melons would slide and had to sometimes be restacked. After a while, everyone got into a rhythm, and if someone dropped a watermelon, everyone became unsynchronized and the driver had to stop the truck. Whenever the driver had to stop because of a mistossed watermelon, he sometimes became very angry and would yell at the culprit.

I was only a small boy, but I stood toe-to-toe with muscular grown men who seemed to have been made of steel. Many of them were built like professional bodybuilders. Some of them resented the fact that I was working side-by-side with them and would sometimes tease me, insult me, and toss watermelons toward me in a tumbling fashion so that they would be hard to catch. They would sometimes throw the watermelon directly at my chest so that it would knock the wind out of me. I had the wind knocked out of me on many occasions. It was not unusual for watermelons to weigh forty or more pounds. Many of the workers were nice and easy to work with, but some were mean-spirited and macho and probably viewed me as a little punk trying to do a man's job.

By growing up in the South and doing hard work, almost all black males had a solid musculature, and there were very few obese people. Being direct descendants of slavery, I'm sure the farmers saw us as A1 specimens. I remember going to the watermelon field, and there must have been about twenty to twenty-five young black males on this white farmer's property, and for some reason, we were unable to harvest the watermelons this particular day. I remember the white farmer saying to the lead black man who was responsible for us, "There are too many niggers out here." It was interesting how grown black men could be demeaned but were helpless to do or say anything.

Many white farmers knew my father, and they all thought well of him. After harvesting the main watermelon crops that were shipped to all parts of the country, the farmers would allow my father to come into their fields and gather the remaining melons. This was a gift to him, and he usually loaded up his truck several times and would sell the melons on the street. It was not unusual for our front yard to be full of watermelons. I remember people coming by at all times of the day and night to buy watermelons from my father. He sold the watermelons for $0.25 to $1.00.

In spite of Alabama being the "cradle of segregation and discrimination" at that time, I always felt that many of the white people had good hearts. This was exemplified by all of the good things I saw them do for my father and other people as well. Because of the deep history of black-white relations in the South, I've always felt that blacks and whites in the South are much closer to each other than they realize.

After harvesting potatoes and watermelons, we also harvested corn, cucumbers, and cantaloupes. For some reason, not as many people were involved in the harvesting of these crops as there were for Irish potatoes and watermelons. As a small boy who was curious about everything, I remember seeing acres and acres of cornfields. I would argue with my older brother, saying that the corn was sugarcane, and it was a long time before I knew the difference. Because we lived in the Deep South, for a long time I thought that we lived in South America.

While working in the cornfields, it was very easy to lose your sense of direction, and it was very scary if you became separated from a group of people you were with. As the wind blew through the cornfield, it produced a noise that sounded like someone was vigorously shaking the corn stalks and chasing after you. Being disoriented in a cornfield is like being lost in the deepest part of a forest.

As a young boy, between the ages of six and twelve years old, along with my brothers, we worked many different jobs. I'm appalled and amazed at how the kids of today complain about taking garbage out or having to make their bed. In addition to having to work all day in ninety-five to one-hundred-degree weather, we labored like grown men at many jobs. My father did not like us sleeping during the day, and one of his favorite sayings was "Nothing comes to a sleeper but dreams." I don't think I ever saw him sleep past 7:00 a.m., even on weekends. My father did so many different things until it's difficult to know where to start. He always felt that an "idle mind was a devil's workshop," so he believed in keeping his sons and daughters busy.

Because of the hard work that he did, he was in perfect health, and we followed his lead in being A1 specimens. He was not afraid to climb to the very top of the tallest pine tree in the state of Alabama. He not only trimmed branches, but he would oftentimes remove entire trees from the roots on up. Our job was to help him with trimming and cutting the trees down and cutting the wood up to be sold as firewood. Many white people and black people in the community had fireplaces and the wood had to be cut to fit their fireplaces. This was very tedious work, not only because we had to use an ax to cut it, but we also had to use a hand saw, and a certain rhythm had to occur when sawing opposite my father. If you could not keep up with him while using the hand saw, he was not pleased. He also had a flatbed truck that he used to deliver the firewood, and we loaded the wood in cords. Many white people who lived in mansions along Mobile Bay liked to burn their fireplaces, especially during the Christmas holidays. Usually on Christmas Eve, people would be calling all day for wood orders. The most popular types of wood to burn were oak and pine.

This was also the pecan season, and many of the white people had acres and acres of pecan trees. We also had several in our yard that yielded yearly crops, and this was how I made extra money during the winter months. There were places in Fairhope that were called pecan sheds. After harvesting pecans, we could take them to the shed, and they would weigh them and pay you a certain amount per pound for them. I oftentimes would use my money to buy my own clothes, school supplies, and when I got older, I remember buying my special girl a Valentine candy.

One day while picking pecans, I was bitten on the neck by a big spider, and my neck became swollen very fast. An elderly black woman took some snuff from out of her mouth and put it on my neck, and the swelling went down.

After working hard all day, I remember the good meals that my mother would have ready when we came home from the fields. I can still taste her blackberry dumplings, butter-baked sweet potatoes, greens, fried chicken, corn bread, dressing, bread pudding, banana pudding, fried corn, okra, string beans, pound cake, and the best fruit cake in the world at Christmastime.

At Christmastime, I never could figure out where the toys were kept. My mother did a very good job of hiding them. We had a tradition of going to church on Christmas morning at around 4:00 or 5:00 a.m. The church was right in front of our house, so we walked and I always remember that the same star appeared in the eastern sky, and this intrigued me because as a kid, I always believed that this star only appeared at Christmas and that it was the star that the Three Kings followed to Bethlehem.

Each year at the same time, the neighbors' roosters crowed, and there was something magical and mystical about this as well. As a kid, I thought that the roosters were letting us know that it was Christmas morning. My mother usually stayed up all night Christmas Eve cooking, and when we returned home from church, she had all of the gifts and toys out. Christmas was a special time of year and the time leading up to Christmas was hectic, but people enjoyed it more than they do today. The true meaning of Christmas was there, and people truly loved one another. I also remember a white, bearded Santa came out to the black area of Fairhope, and from atop his fire truck, he would throw down brown paper bags filled with fruit, candy, and a toy to the black kids. What was strange about this was that he threw the bags down, but he never came down from the truck.

After the Christmas season, we continued to harvest pecans and other crops. Again, my father would climb to the top of pecan trees and shake the branches so as to make the pecans fall. The month of January can get cold in Alabama, and my father would build a fire in the middle of the pecan field, and this is how we stayed warm. The white farmers would pay us five cents a pound for all of the pecans we picked and he oftentimes received a lot more per pound when he sold them at the local pecan shed.

Many of the local farmers used posts for fencing, and my father would split the wood, skin it with a special tool, and sell it to the farmers. He taught me and my brothers how to skin the bark off the wood in a rounded fashion. People also contracted with him to tear down houses, and he would sell the lumber to whoever would buy it. We had to pile the lumber in special places according to the length and width of the wood. We also had to use a crowbar and a hammer to remove all of the nails and sort them according to sizes. As kids, we stepped on many rusty nails, but we never considered the possibility of contracting tetanus. We also learned how to collect turpentine from pine trees. This was very sticky work, and the resin from the pine tree could be extremely hard to remove from your clothing as well as your skin. Certain parts of the pine tree, and especially the trunk, burn like gasoline and can be used as a fire starter.

One black person in the community was a chicken farmer. He had thousands of chickens and sold some of the chickens to residents in the area, and his eggs were sold to stores and to local residents. One embarrassing moment for me was when my father was hired to remove the chicken manure. Again, he brought us along with shovels and boots to transfer what seemed like tons of chicken manure onto his truck for transfer to farmers and other people who wanted to buy it for fertilization for pecan trees, tomato plants, flowers, and other plants. It seemed that my father always had a plan of how to make money in more ways than one, and we were not always privy to what he was thinking. We were also right along with him when he collected iron, copper, and steel to take to the junkyard in Mobile. No one was overweight because we were always working. Today, kids are overweight because they tend to eat all of the wrong foods and they're extremely inactive. If many of the kids today did the work that I did as a child, they would probably die from exhaustion.

We were surrounded by soybean farmers, but I never understood the nature of soybeans and what they were used for. Cotton fields were sparse at that time, but now there is a resurgence of them. We were surrounded by many fruits and vegetables, and we harvested sweet potatoes, cucumbers, blackberries, wild grapes, satsumas (tangerines), corn, Japanese plums, huckleberries, and persimmons.

While picking blackberries, I often ran into snakes, and the elders would often say that some snakes could outrun you. I remember picking blackberries one day, and if I had not looked down, I would have stepped on a large black snake that was curled up with its head in the air. After seeing the snake, I ran all the way home. As I cut through a farmer's field, I crawled under some barbwire, and it snagged my clothing and I temporarily panicked. Even though I was far away from the snake, I felt that it was right behind me, and while caught in the barbwire, my imagination was telling me that the snake was there. Picking blackberries was another way for me to make money because I would sell them by the quart to local women in the community.

To this day, I have never tasted anyone's blackberry dumpling that tasted better than my mother's. Wild mushrooms grew all over the place, but my mother always cautioned us about poison mushrooms so I never touched them. Almost everyone had a garden, and people would swap vegetables or they would simply tell you to go out in the garden and pick whatever you wanted. Also, in front of our house stood a mulberry tree. A mulberry looks exactly like a long worm, and sometimes the worm could be camouflaged to look just like the mulberry. The mulberry is also a berry that can leave an indelible stain on your hands and clothing. We also had two fig trees, pear trees, and all of the women canned pears and other fruits and vegetables. My mother made homemade biscuits, and the figs, pears, and wild grapes that she preserved (canned) were very delicious with hot biscuits. My father would boil the rind of a watermelon, sweeten it, and this would be canned as well. I'm not sure where this idea came from, but my guess is that this may have been something that the slaves did.

During the summer months, I remember walking for miles without shoes on. We walked on the hot pavement, and you could see the heat rising above the pavement. At certain times of the day, the pavement felt like it was 110 degrees. Sometimes the gravel, and the hot tar together would stick to your skin and become lodged between your toes. The heat and the continued pounding of our feet on the pavement caused blisters to our feet that we became accustomed to it. We also ended up with a stubbed big toe on many occasions. I guess, as kids, we just felt fortunate that we had a pavement to walk on because for many years, the pavement stopped in the area where black people lived. This was also true for street lights. If a person has not lived through racial oppression and discrimination, it is extremely difficult to imagine man's inhumanity to man.

When I attended school in Alabama, the schools were completely segregated. I remember when Governor George C. Wallace stood in the doorway of the University of Alabama to prevent black students from entering. He was a staunch segregationist as all of the governors before him were. As long as black people knew "their place," many white people were satisfied. Governor George C. Wallace, along with many other white people, would have done anything to have prevented race-mixing. In my mind, the bottom line was to, at all costs, keep the black man away from the white woman. Because of these racial attitudes, the schools became separate and unequal, and we had two societies, one black and one white, separate and unequal.

In spite of having to attend a separate and unequal school, starting in first grade, I feel that we had black teachers who were qualified to teach. They were also caring, and they also taught us to strive for excellence in everything we did. As black men and women, they endured racism, discrimination, humiliation, and degradation in its worse form. When you think of it, they were only about two generations from slavery.

In 2008, Alabama governor Bob Riley signed a resolution expressing profound regret for Alabama's role and apologized for slavery's long and lingering effects.

Mr. Alvin Boykin was the principal of Anna T. Jeanes, the local elementary school. He was a man of honor and integrity, and he was also a task master. In addition to his school duties, he was deeply religious and he helped everyone in the community. When all of the teachers had gone home, it was not unusual to see a light on in his office at 9:00 or 10:00 p.m. at night. All of the teachers knew the struggles that we would have to face growing up as black children in the South. They knew the ugly face of racism, but they were helpless to do anything about it. If a black teacher had tried to enter a white restaurant, they would not have been served or they would have been arrested. I still marvel at the inner strength, faith, and hope that my teachers, parents, and other adults had in dealing with such blatant and overt racism. The poem "Invictus" exemplifies the courage and the strength of all the people who came before us to open the doors for this generation and generations to come:

"Invictus"
William Ernest Henley

Out of the night that covers me.
Black as the pit from pole to pole,
I thank whatever Gods may be
For my unconquerable soul.
In the fell clutch of circumstance
I have not winced nor cried aloud.
Under the bludgeoning of chance
My head is bloody, but unbowed.
Beyond this place of wrath and tears
Looms but the Horror of the shade,
And yet the menace of the years
Finds and shall find me unafraid.

DR. EARL BRACY

> It matters not how strait the gate,
> How charged with punishment the scroll,
> I am the master of my fate:
> I am the captain of my soul.

In addition to being the principal of Anna T. Jeanes School, Mr. Boykin was also the leader of the Boy Scouts. As students, we had to recite the Pledge of Allegiance on a daily basis. As children, at that time, we did not understand that this was a tremendous contradiction. We lived in a society that deliberately kept black people oppressed, marginalized, and out of the mainstream. In spite of being stripped of his dignity as a black, educated man, Mr. Boykin, our principal, always picked several students on a daily basis to raise and lower the American flag. At the end of the day, we would also fold the flag in the meticulous manner in which it was to be folded. White people would sometimes stop their cars and watch us as we methodically folded the flag. Our principal knew that his worth as a black man was diminished, but this did not deter him from being patriotic to a country and a state that would have killed him if he became too vocal and too militant. He was put on this earth for a purpose, and he taught us valuable lessons in having patience, humility, determination, and perseverance. His wife, Mrs. Ida Boykin, was an elementary teacher who was attractive, distinguished, and a no-nonsense person. She lived a long life, and my mother informed me that she died during the month of September 2009. It saddens me even now that all of these talented and highly educated teachers could not sit down at a nice seafood restaurant and have dinner because of racial discrimination and the malice that some whites had against blacks.

Anna T. Jeanes School also had an annex that was approximately a quarter of a mile away. This school was a large wooden building that had several coal-operated heaters. One Saturday morning, we saw flames gushing from this building from where we lived. The fire engines were roaring to go and put this fire out, but the fire spread too fast and the school was destroyed in a matter of minutes. Rumor had it that a white man was seen around the school that morning, but this was never proven. As I watched in disbelief from a distance as the fire burned, I will never forget a teacher who, I think, taught the third grade at the time. As she traveled in her car at a very slow speed on the road on which we lived, she could look to her right across an open field that belonged to Mr. Angelo Houston and see the flames as they roared into the atmosphere at a height that was no match for the city fire department. The vivid memory of the look on my teacher's face as she saw these flames has forever been etched in my memory. I will never forget the tears streaming down her face as she looked into massive flames as the fire department stood helpless.

The same teacher, whose name was Mrs. Willie Carter, was also a pianist, and whenever we would have assembly, she would play what was probably her favorite song, "I Come to the Garden Alone" by C. Austin Miles. The words are as follows:

> I come to the garden alone
> While the dew is still on the roses
> And the voice I hear falling on my ear
> The Son of God discloses.
>
> And He walks with me, and He talks with me,
> And He tells me I am His own;
> And the joy we share as we tarry there,
> None other has ever known.
>
> He speaks, and the sound of His voice,
> Is so sweet the birds hush their singing,
> And the melody that He gave to me
> Within my heart is ringing.
>
> I'd stay in the garden with Him
> Though the night around me be falling,
> But He bids me go; through the voice of woe
> His voice to me is calling.

Anna T. Jeanes School was founded and financed by a Quaker by the name of Ms. Anna T. Jeanes. She was a wealthy lady from

Philadelphia who established a fund to build schools for African Americans in the South. At that time, the words to use for African American were *Negro* or *colored*.

As a young boy, we did not have much, but almost every black child had their father and mother. Men generally did not leave their families, and even though some were alcoholics, they were there. Many young black boys and young men emulated the behaviors of their father and became alcoholics as well. Older blacks in particular and some younger blacks tended to be subservient to white people. Many of them dealt with the sting of discrimination, racism, and oppression by dampening the pain with alcohol. They seemed to have been at the mercy of any white person, and even though they were hurting, they kept smiling. Many black people wore a mask as Paul Laurence Dunbar said in his poem, "We Wear the Mask":

>We wear the mask that grins and lies,
>It hides our cheeks and shades our eyes—
>This debt we pay to human guile;
>With torn and bleeding hearts we smile,
>And mouth with myriad subtleties.
>
>Why should the world be over-wise,
>In counting all our tears and sighs?
>Nay, let them only see us, while
>We wear the mask.
>
>We smile, but, O great Christ, our cries
>To thee from tortured souls arise.
>We sing, but oh the clay is vile
>Beneath our feet, and long the mile;
>But let the world dream otherwise,
>We wear the mask!

Growing up in Fairhope, Alabama, was interesting because even though we were residents of Fairhope, we were not really true citizens. We were invisible, marginalized, and expected to always be in a position of subserviency. As a young black boy, I remember watching *The Edge of Night*, but I could never understand why there was so much skipping from part to part. There were no black characters in *The Edge of Night* unless they were maids, cleaning furniture, babysitting, or washing dishes. It was also mandatory that the maid wore a uniform. As far as I can recall, there were three television stations in the area: two in Mobile and one in Pensacola, Florida, which was a forty-five-minute drive.

Channel 5 in Mobile played cartoons in the afternoon, and sometimes the station would have large groups of kids at the station on certain days, and the kids would be interviewed between cartoons. The television anchor person had a great time engaging the kids, and the kids were funny and candid. What was even more interesting was that the black kids came to the station one day, and the white kids came on a different day. It was an unwritten law that they would never mingle. This type of maltreatment can leave an indelible psychological scar on its victims.

At least 99.9 percent or more of the black people in Fairhope had no dental or health insurance. People usually went to the dentist if they needed a tooth extracted, and no one knew anything about preventive care. If we had dental problems, our father would take us three towns over to a white dentist because he was the only white dentist who would take black patients. This dentist's office was in Robertsdale, Alabama.

In spite of the humiliation, our community was always buzzing with activity. It seemed like everyone had a special talent for something. I can still hear the sounds of saw blades, chickens, ducks, cows, hogs, owls, crickets, frogs, laughter, children playing, and fog horns coming from boats on Mobile Bay.

Since seafood was plentiful, people were always having crab boils and fish fries. The men in the community would butcher hogs and smoke fish quite a bit. They would take an old refrigerator, make a fire at the bottom of it, and put the fish on its shelves with the door closed and smoke the fish until they were palatable.

All of the adults were addressed by their proper names. As children, we never called any adult by their first name. Even though I have four degrees, I still call the adults in my hometown Mr. or Mrs. They still call me Earl, and it is not important that I be addressed as Doctor.

When I was in the ninth grade, I wanted to be a journalist and that thought faded, but with all of the writing that I do, maybe it never faded. When I was also in the ninth grade, I remember my grandmother walking into our house and saying to my mother, "I can look at Earl's forehead and tell that he's going to be successful." I don't know what she saw, but her statement always stuck with me.

As a kid, I was always industrious and found many ways to make money. I read hundreds to thousands of comic books and ads. One day I ordered some live baby chickens (chicks) via regular mail. Someone from the post office called me one day and told me that I had some chickens at the post office, and if I wanted them, I needed to get to the post office right away because half of them were dead. I think I ordered about one hundred of them, and about forty-five or more were dead. I also used to order medicinal salve, and I would sell it to some of the women in the community.

My father did not look down on anyone. If a drunk was walking along the highway, he would even bring them home and my mother would feed them. Even though we were considered poor, there were others who were poorer and my father uplifted them every day. He displayed the image of God in his life. He was mostly quiet and unassuming, but when he walked into the pulpit, the Holy Spirit took over.

When people became sick in the community, they all called on my father to pray for them. His prayers were powerful, and they were genuine and from the heart. Some people in the community did not go to church at all and others were from other denominations, but they had no problem asking him for prayer. Even with four degrees and three and a half years of lay ministry training, I will never know the Bible as well and as thorough as my father knew it. He attended Sunday school, midday service, during the week, and church on Sunday nights. He also had no problem dropping to his knees to pray. When he talked about heaven, he would say that heaven was a place of milk and honey. I didn't fully understand the expression, and I said to myself, if they drink just milk and honey every day, I don't want to go there.

My mother was very spontaneous when it came to playing the piano or the organ. It did not matter what time of day it was; when the spirit hit her, she would start playing and sometimes it would be for hours. Oftentimes people would come by the house just to hear her play. She had many special songs, but two that I remember were "Blessed Assurance" and "I'm Pressing On."

Many other strong people came before us, and they never got a chance to know what freedom was. They sacrificed their lives so that we could have a better life, and we must not forget to pay homage to them in all that we do. There are also many black graves in Fairhope that are without headstones, and this we must correct.

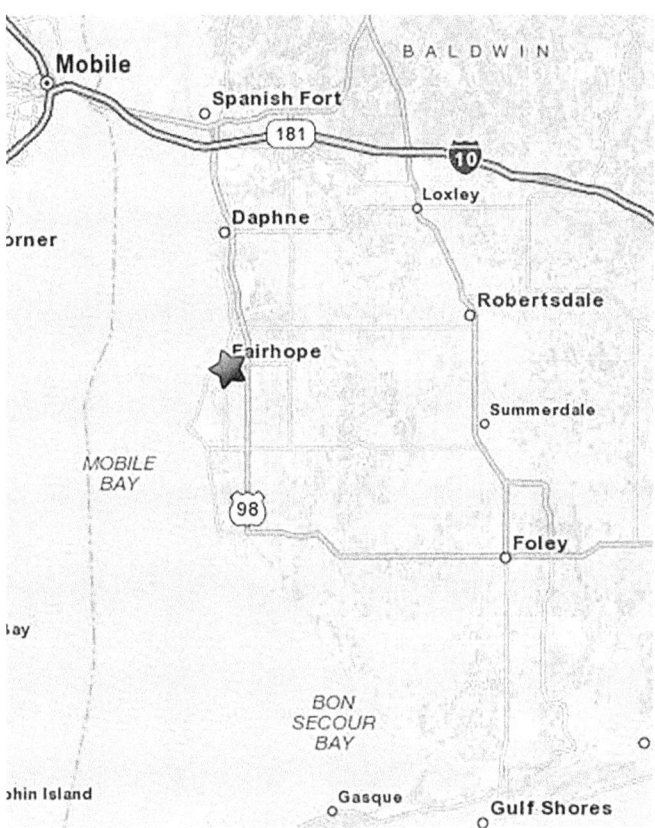

Fairhope, Alabama, is a tourist town that sits on Mobile Bay, a tributary of the Gulf of Mexico.

A replica of a slave ship found at the bottom of the Atlantic Ocean

THE MAKING OF A BLACK PSYCHOLOGIST

My father sitting on the porch of the home in which I was born

A new family home was built in 1988.

My parent's wedding over sixty years ago in Cantonment, Florida

My mother playing the piano after her eighty-fifth birthday party

My brothers and I sat on the back porch of this home belonging to a white family when President Eisenhower ordered federal troops into Little Rock, Arkansas, to protect nine black students. We played and broke bread with the white family's kids.

It was common to see signs posted near piers that read Whites Only.

My father was also a tree trimmer, and he oftentimes climbed to the top of the tallest pine trees in Alabama.

Daphne, Alabama, is adjacent to the town of Fairhope and is known as Jubilee City because of the jubilee.

This black church sits along Highway 98 near Mobile Bay and the old high school. It is also as old as the majestic pine and oak trees that surround it.

Little Bethel Baptist Church is a historic landmark that is kept immaculately clean.

The lady in the middle was my first-grade teacher, Mrs. Ida Holt. To the left of her is my sister.

The Grand Hotel Marriott, which also sits on Mobile Bay

An Alabama Irish potato field

A country store where we bought lunch.
As of 2010, this store still stands.

A deadly ant bed

A watermelon patch

A pecan orchard where I spent many hours and days

My mother in her kitchen, where she loved to cook

This fire truck sits in the Fairhope Museum. It is one of the same fire trucks that Santa sat atop.

A cotton field in Baldwin County, Alabama

Governor George C. Wallace stood in the doorway of the University of Alabama to prevent black students from entering in the mid to late 1960s.

George Wallace, governor of Alabama during the turbulent 1960s

Anna T. Jeanes Elementary School

This is the main highway (Section Street) that separated blacks and whites in Fairhope. My father also cleared this main thoroughfare with an ax and a handsaw when he first came to the town of Fairhope.

Offensive street names still exist in Fairhope as of 2010.

This is the new municipal swimming pool. As children, we were not permitted to swim in the pool at all.

CHAPTER TWO

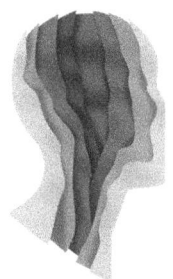

Living in Oak Creek, Wisconsin (A Culture Shock)

As I stated previously, I came from a very large family where there were six boys and six girls. One of my father's brothers, Mr. Wilmer Matherson, lived in Oak Creek, Wisconsin, which is a suburb of Milwaukee. My uncle and his wife did not have any children of their own, and my uncle asked if one of the boys could come and live with them. As fate would have it, I volunteered for the journey. My father brought me to Milwaukee on a Greyhound bus, and I remember the trip being quite exciting as we stopped in many of the major cities traveling north. Upon arriving at the bus station in Milwaukee, my uncle drove in from Oak Creek, Wisconsin, to pick us up.

What was apparent to me immediately was that there was a drastic drop in the temperature, especially for the month of June. In Alabama, in June at 7:00 a.m., it is normal to experience a temperature of eighty-five degrees. On the contrary, upon arriving in Milwaukee, the temperature was in the low fifties at 7:00 a.m. Also, the weather could also change drastically at any given minute. This encounter was my first culture shock. The city of Oak Creek lies right on Lake Michigan, and we were three-fourths of a mile from the lake.

I was also soon to discover that only three black families lived in Oak Creek at that time, and when I arrived there, I was twelve years old. To my amazement, I could not drink the water because of the taste and the smell. Being that water is an important element, my uncle and aunt had to find a way to entice me to drink it. Boiling the water worked because this made it more palatable.

Before my father returned back to Alabama, his first question to me was, "Earl, are you sure you want to do this?" I did have mixed feelings, but I did not want to disappoint my uncle and aunt. My uncle took to me right away, and if I had said, "No, I do not want to stay," I felt that I would have disappointed him.

In leaving, going back to Alabama, my father voiced one request of his brother. His request was, "Make sure Earl goes to church every Sunday." My uncle and aunt were not churchgoing people, but the next-door neighbors were black and they attended Greater Galilee Church in Milwaukee. I attended church with them, and I didn't mind going because they had two boys who were similar in age to me. My uncle worked for the Oak Creek Power Plant, and he owned his own construction company, and as a matter of fact, he built his own home and he could build any type of room.

One night the Oak Creek Police Department dispatched two police officers to my uncle's home, and many months passed before my aunt shared with me the nature of the visit. She informed me that someone had called the house and stated, "If any more niggers move in, we're going to bomb your house and theirs too." I think that I was oblivious to it all because I had made friends at school with a variety of kids whose nationalities varied, and for some reason, it was hard for me to see racial prejudice and hatred in the same light as my uncle and aunt saw it.

Even though I had grown up in the segregated South, my naivete led me to believe that people were good, and if they smiled at you, they must like you. My uncle tried to give me the hard facts about racial prejudice because I think he knew that I needed to have a tough hide so to speak. I truly believed that he did not want me to go through what he went through as a black man. He stressed education and he always wanted me to be a medical doctor. My uncle also took a leap of faith when he acted as a maverick in leaving his comfort zone to build a home in an exclusively white environment. This experience was beneficial to me because it allowed me to leave my comfort zone of an all-black school in my native Alabama and acclimate to an environment where I, for the first time, attended school with Hispanic, Irish, Polish, German, Italian, Danish, Amish, Hungarian, and many other students. Even though I was called a nigger on more than one occasion, my overall experience was positive.

While on the playground one day, a student called me a nigger and ran, and as he ran up the stairs and into the classroom, I chased him, and as he entered the door way, I caught up with him and kicked him in the rear end. My uncle had already prepared me for the verbal insults and he encouraged me to not be a coward. The teacher, Mrs. Kinow, saw me kick the other student, and she wanted to know what happened because she could see that I was visibly upset. She was a teacher who was fair and firm, and because of this incident, she lectured the entire class on the impact of racial slurs and respecting individual differences. She also made the other student apologize to me, and she reprimanded him for quite some time.

While living in Oak Creek, Wisconsin, for three years, I attended Meadowview Elementary School, Greenlawn Junior High School, and Oak Creek Junior High School. One thing happened that was a blow to my self-esteem, and that was that because I was a black student coming from rural Alabama, the principal made a decision to put me back in the sixth grade when I should have been in the seventh. I stayed in sixth grade for almost a month, and they decided to move me into my right grade because my teacher discovered that I could do the work.

Also, when it was time to take the national exams that are given every year, it was discovered that even though I was black and from the South, I received the highest scores in my class in reading and vocabulary. I was also the only black student in my class. Because of the scores I received, the principal wanted to know who sat to my left, my right, in front of me, and behind me, and after I gave him this information, he made me stay after school and take the test again. This time he put me in a room by myself with the door open, and he walked by about every minute. After the test was scored, nothing changed. I received the same exact scores. While in the seventh grade, I was also reading on a twelfth-grade level.

On another occasion, my English literature teacher stood up in front of the class and told the class that when I first came to her class, she thought that I was too dumb to spell my own name. She went on to report that she had read a paper that I had written for class, on Robert Louis Stevenson's *Treasure Island*. I received an A+ on the paper, and her comment to the class was, "But he's not stupid like I thought, he's brilliant." It's interesting that her comment did not make me feel any better, but instead, I felt a diminishment in my self-worth. It is important that teachers be very sensitive about what they say to students. Also, a teacher can make or break a student. Even though I was a black student from rural Alabama and I was in sixth grade, I was reading on a twelfth-grade level. That can also be attributed to my mother reading to us at an early age and the expertise and the dedication of strong black teachers in the South who graduated from historically black colleges and universities.

After a while, I sensed that my uncle may have been concerned about my safety. He bought me a set of boxing gloves and we would spar together. He taught me how to position my feet, how to follow my opponent, how to defend myself from a punch, and how to throw a devastating punch. After learning all of those techniques, I discovered that I also possessed a great deal of raw talent. Many times I would take my boxing gloves to school and attempt to engage other students. It was difficult to find students who would box me because I had a reputation of throwing combination punches that would send my opponent to the floor. One of the teachers was determined to have the best athlete at school box me during a gym period. This bout took place, and I remember vividly beating the star athlete (David) so badly until his face, gloves, and shirt were drenched with blood. His girlfriend was screaming because he was being beaten so badly, but he kept pursuing me and the teacher would not stop the fight. Finally, the teacher did stop the fight, and he gently whispered in my ear, "When you're beating a guy that bad, you should just stop fighting on your own." I always felt that he somehow wanted David to either knock me down or knock me out.

As a black kid growing up in Oak Creek, I would oftentimes put my boxing gloves on my handle bars of my bicycle and ride around looking for someone to box. I even rode into neighboring communities, but sometimes kids would see me coming and go inside. After a while, I started feeling dejected because after all, why have boxing gloves if you can only use them on a punching bag?

Coming to Wisconsin also exposed me to ice-skating. There was a nearby pond in the neighborhood that stayed frozen most of the winter, and this is where I learned to skate. Other times my uncle would take me into Milwaukee to various skating rinks. He was a big proponent of being involved in the YMCA, and I spent many Saturdays at the YMCA (Northside) in Milwaukee, where I boxed, lifted weights, and swam.

In the eighth grade, we had school dances during the day, and one of my classmates who I thought was very pretty asked me to slow dance. I vaguely remember the song being "The Treasure of Love." I'm not sure who took the lead, but we were dancing cheek to cheek as eighth graders (smile). The same male teacher who had me box David stood almost between us as we danced as if he was the referee. I guess he felt as if he needed to chaperone.

During this same period in my life at the age of thirteen, I was a very active thirteen-year-old. One day, as I was riding my bike, I came in the house with a severe stomachache. As it became worse, my uncle and aunt took me into Milwaukee to their family doctor.

After examining me, I was told that I had stomach flu and was sent home with medication. That same night, things got worse medically, and the doctor told my uncle to bring me to the emergency room right away. On the initial examination, the doctor was unable to detect any rebound tenderness in my lower right quadrant of my abdomen because when I was examined, I pretended as if there was no pain there. The pain was severe, and if I had told the doctor the first time, he would have known that I had appendicitis. When I was taken to surgery, my appendix had ruptured, which could have been potentially life-threatening. Because of my dishonesty in describing my symptoms, I ended up in the hospital for fourteen days and lost about fourteen pounds. To this day, I feel that my life was spared, and I was protected by a higher power other than the doctors and nurses who took care of me.

There was also a negative side to living with my uncle and aunt. They never had children of their own, and I did not always feel comfortable in their home, even though they would have given me the world. The love and discipline that came from my parents was different. I always felt that there was always this coalition formed between them (my uncle and aunt) against me. They did not always understand me, and many times I don't think they really tried to. If there was a disagreement in my uncle and aunt's home, I felt a tremendous amount of tension that lasted for days and this was sometimes chronic. This was the complete opposite in my parents' home in Alabama. Even though there were eleven other siblings, whenever my parents disciplined me or any of my siblings, there was still a sense of love and peace in the house. My father was a minister, and my mother was the church organist and pianist, and in spite of any disagreement with any of their children, we knew that the love and caring were there.

Coming from a very religious family, I always listened to my father talk about the second coming of Christ. As a twelve-year-old who was a thousand miles from home, I also had spiritual thoughts that bothered me, such as what if Jesus made his second return and I was not with my family?

We all have our schemas and belief systems in accordance to who we're modeling. I would oftentimes hear my father say, "At the second coming of Christ, there would be a bright light in the sky." As a twelve-year-old, I was very conflicted about how this would happen and when it would happen. I bring this topic up because one night my uncle and aunt called me outside to view a bright light in the sky. It was exciting to them, but in my mind, I wasn't sure what the light represented. When I saw the bright light, I immediately became frightened and ran to the bedroom thinking that it was the end of the world biblically speaking. My uncle and aunt did not understand why I decided to hide because they did not understand my upbringing and I did not discuss this with them. Both my uncle and aunt thought that I didn't care about anything, and they ridiculed me for being disinterested and indifferent about natural occurring phenomena. What they were looking at were the northern lights or aurora borealis. Coming from the South, I had never heard of the northern lights. While living in Oak Creek, I also spent part of the summer and weekends with my other uncle and aunt, Mr. Claude Matherson and Mrs. Mae Matherson, who lived in Milwaukee. Their home was always open to me, and they always showed me a tremendous amount of love.

I made the decision to return to Alabama to finish high school, and this was a very good decision. I was also able to bring my boxing gloves with me, but I had to leave my ice skates behind. The rationale that my aunt gave was that "There's no ice in Alabama."

As a psychologist, I oftentimes see many foster children who may be the only child in the home but who chose to return to their family of origin. In many cases, they may receive more amenities in the foster home but choose to be with their biological family. Likewise, I made my choice, and it was to be with my biological family in Alabama. We are where we are supposed to be at any given time in life, and I am absolutely sure that the time spent with my uncle and aunt in Oak Creek, Wisconsin, was part of the plan in order for me to complete my assigned tasks as I continue to travel this planet.

The home that my uncle built from the ground up in Oak Creek, Wisconsin

I attended Meadowview Elementary School in sixth grade before being put in my proper grade.

I attended seventh grade at Greenlawn Junior High School in Oak Creek. The school was eventually torn down, and this area is now Greenlawn Park.

I attended Oak Creek Junior High, which was expanded and turned into Oak Creek High School. I was the first black student at Oak Creek Junior High School.

CHAPTER THREE

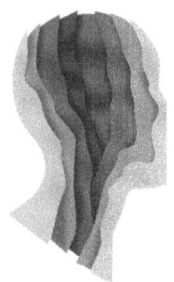

High School Years in the Segregated South

After leaving Oak Creek Middle School in Oak Creek, Wisconsin, I traveled back to my hometown of Fairhope, Alabama, to attend high school. As mentioned earlier, black students were not allowed to attend the local high school in Fairhope, and instead, all black students attended the black school in Daphne, Alabama (Baldwin County Training School). My great, great uncle Reverend S. B. Bracy was the founder of this school. After returning to Fairhope, Alabama, from Oak Creek, Wisconsin, I was somewhat a changed person. My family and people in the community told me that I talked "proper." I did not see myself as talking "proper," but I guess the change process can be insidious. When I lived in Oak Creek, Wisconsin, I was accustomed to having my own everything. It was hard for me to share a bedroom, and to this very day, my brothers and sisters remind me of my nuances and idiosyncratic behaviors. It took me a while to become reacclimated to my own family.

While in high school, I worked in two different restaurants. I worked at one restaurant called the Parker House Restaurant and Hotel, owned by Mr. Lee Parker and his wife. Mr. Parker was a white man who had a good heart, but at the same time, he went along with the segregationist laws of Alabama. His wife was a small, pleasant lady who was an excellent cook, and her sweet potato pies, coconut pies, lemon pies, and pecan pies were the "bomb." She was stern but she and her husband were fond of me. All of his waitresses were white, and they were fond of me as well. They all knew that I was a good student, and they wanted me to do well.

The white chief of police was a good friend of Mr. Parker's, and he made many trips to the restaurant for coffee and meals. I was always uncomfortable around him because he always stared at me but would never smile. His wife made good fried apple and peach turnovers, and she would bring in special batches for me. I did find out later that Mr. Parker was boasting about me to all of the white dignitaries who came into his restaurant. He was a good cook himself, and he enjoyed cooking hush puppies, fried oysters, meat loaf, pork chops, biscuits, and a host of other foods. His restaurant never closed on Sundays, and he prepared his best meals on that day.

Every Sunday at about 12:30 p.m., his restaurant was filled to capacity with people coming from church. I had to clean tables and bring out clean silverware and glasses to the main dining area, and sometimes I felt invisible. Oftentimes, the white people continued their conversations while I cleaned tables, and I felt like a nonperson. When I came out into the dining area one Sunday, an elderly white man said to me, "Boy, go bring me a screwdriver." I had no idea that there was a drink called a screwdriver. I brought back a screwdriver (a tool), and he looked at me and screamed to the top of his voice, "Boy, that's not a got damn screwdriver."

At that point, I felt like running out of the restaurant because I felt like everyone was looking at me in amazement for being so stupid. From the expressions on their faces, it did not seem like they felt sorry for this sixteen-year-old kid who did not know that a screwdriver was vodka and orange juice. Mrs. Parker did try to console me later, but in spite of her consoling me, I had been deeply wounded. When white people came in on Sundays, they seemed somber and serious because of their belief in segregation. I used to ask, as Martin Luther King did, "Who was their God? Did they truly believe that Heaven was going to be segregated?"

In Martin Luther King's letter from Birmingham jail, he wrote, "I have traveled the length and breadth of Alabama, Mississippi, and all the other southern states. On sweltering summer days and crisp autumn mornings, I have looked at her beautiful churches with their lofty spires, pointing heavenward. I have beheld the impressive outlay of her massive religious education buildings. Over and over again, I have found myself asking: What kind of people worship here? Who is their God? Where were their voices when the lips of Governor Barnett dripped with words of interposition and nullification? Where were they when Governor Wallace gave the clarion call for defiance and hatred? Where were their voices of support when tired, bruised, and weary Negro men and women decided to rise from the dark dungeons of complacency to the bright hills of creative protest? Oh, how we have blemished and scarred the body of Christ, through social neglect and fear of being nonconformists."

No blacks could come in with their families and sit down and enjoy a Sunday dinner without having the police called. Although I cleaned the dining area every night, I had to eat in the back, and when I came to work, I had to enter through the back door. This was commonplace throughout the South, and it was also an unwritten rule. I also cleaned the male and female bathrooms in the dining room every night, but I had to use a bathroom in the rear of the restaurant that had a commode and a sink and was the same size as a small closet. When the restaurant would close, I had to mop the dining area, clear the tables, clean and mop the kitchen area, and wash all of the dishes, including pots and pans.

If I remember correctly, Mr. Parker liked vodka and tonic, and when the restaurant closed, he would clear out the cash register and fix himself a drink. Some nights he would fix himself three or four drinks. When he was drinking, he would sometimes keep me there standing at the counter, talking to me about many things, which included politics, religion, and many times race. He sometimes would keep me there talking to me until 2:00 a.m. in the morning. I worked many long hours, and sometimes I would work sixty hours per week. During the summer months, I worked a lot more than sixty hours. When Mr. Parker would talk to me at night, I could tell that he had a disdain for Martin Luther King, Ralph Abernathy, and the civil rights movement that was going on in Selma, Alabama. Black people in the town of Fairhope lived in a separate part of town, and whenever Mr. Parker would drink a vodka and tonic, he referred to the black section of town as nigger quarters. This is where I lived, and I was always shocked and appalled whenever he used the words *nigger quarters*. This was very insensitive of him, and if he was using the words *nigger quarters* in front of me, this must have been used by many other white people in everyday talk. I always felt like he thought that the demonstrating and boycotts going on in Selma, Montgomery, and Birmingham would also find their way down to where we lived. This was also a fear that many other white people had as well.

Things were changing in the South, and white people were starting to become fearful. It was very common to see almost every white man in multiple counties in Alabama riding around in their pickup trucks with a rifle in the rear window. As a sixteen-year-old youth, I knew that these rifles were not for hunting deer, but instead, they were visible to intimidate black people.

Another thing that I noticed was that there were many white men who were "volunteer firefighters." When they became a volunteer firefighter, they would mount a flashing red light on the dash of their cars. I always said to myself that the small town of Fairhope did not need that many volunteer firefighters. Again, this was a tactic used as a show of force in containing and controlling black people. Many of these "volunteer firefighters" came into Mr. Parker's restaurant, and I always quietly observed their interactions. In addition to my other duties in the restaurant, I had to peel many potatoes, make potato salad, perform the duties of a short order cook, hose down the concrete outside, and maintain a flower bed in front of the restaurant. The Parker House sat right on Highway 98, which was a scenic route along Mobile Bay. When I was in high school, I did not realize the significance of this highway with all of its magnificent oak trees, it's mansions that sat back from the highway, and the historic markers that went all the way back to the Civil War. This area was great for tourism, and it was common to see cars that had license plates from Texas, Louisiana, Mississippi, and Florida.

While working at the Parker House Restaurant, Mr. Parker hired an eighteen-year-old Caucasian lady from England. She was a brunette who was absolutely beautiful. Her British accent was intriguing, and she had an exceptionally pleasant personality. She had a habit of always wanting to touch me, and she could not understand why black people were treated differently. Interestingly, she was quite bold and she repeatedly asked me to take her out, and I found myself explaining to her the reasons black males did not date white girls in Alabama. Whenever she talked to me, you could see the hurt in her eyes because of the subservience that black people had to relegate themselves to. When I graduated from high school, she went out of her way to buy me extraordinary gifts. I really liked her, but I also knew the consequences if I had acted on my impulses.

Many of the boys who I attended high school with drove their parents' car, but I had my own car throughout high school. The first car I owned was an Oldsmobile Delta 88, and my second car was a Corvair, which no one else had. Mr. Parker was also responsible for me getting the Corvair. He was friends with a local car dealer, and the dealer allowed me to make payments over time.

As a teenager, you also have to be reminded of your responsibility of being a safe driver. One afternoon when I was leaving the school, while driving my Oldsmobile, I turned onto the main highway, which was Highway 98. My Oldsmobile had so much power, if you mashed the accelerator to the floor, the front of the car would lift up and the front wheels felt like they were leaving the ground. This particular day, I decided to peel rubber at a high rate of speed right in front of the school. The next day, a teacher came to me and said, "Earl, I saw what you did yesterday. That was dangerous, and I'm really surprised at you. Those little kids really look up to you as a role model." I never forgot what this teacher said to me, and it was something that I never did again. The elementary school was right next to the high school, and I do remember how the small kids were so excited whenever they saw me.

Like Mr. Parker, of the Parker House Restaurant, all of my teachers expected great things from me. In spite of a segregationist stance, Mr. Parker always pushed education, and he encouraged me. His daughter worked in his restaurant, and she was always cordial and friendly toward me. She eventually went on to college and became a teacher. His son had finished college long before I came there and was an engineer.

I also worked at a restaurant called the Ebb Tide. This restaurant was in the downtown section of Fairhope and about five blocks from the police station. The cooks were black, and the food was excellent. The black employees had to enter through the back door, and the owners of the restaurant were an air force sergeant and his wife. They owned a Cadillac, and the sergeant's wife would pick up the black cook who was our next-door neighbor and bring her to work. The cook was a heavyset lady who bowed down to white people in every sense of the word.

Whenever the "boss" picked her up, she always sat in the back seat, and this was an unwritten rule throughout the South. The cook's name was Ms. Bessie, and Ms. Bessie was careful not to do anything that would upset white people. My duty at the restaurant was dishwasher and bus boy, and the sergeant and his wife were quite fond of me. In spite of their fondness for me, I needed to test the limits. I had become sick and tired of black people having to go to the back door to be served at the restaurants, and I challenged my best friend, Alonzo, by daring him to enter the front door of the restaurant, sit down, and order a meal. He took me up on my dare, and he came into the restaurant, through the front door, which was forbidden, and ordered a meal. The two white waitresses turned every color but black. One of them came in the kitchen and stated, "There's a colored boy sitting out front and he put an order in." In the meantime, they called the police. While the white people were trying to deal with the confusion, Ms. Bessie, the black cook, came into the front of the restaurant and said to my friend, Alonzo, "Lord have mercy Jesus, boy, what you doin' up in these here white folks' restaurant! Oh my god! Oh my god! "I can't remember if Alonzo was served or not, but shortly after he left, the police came and they went looking for him but could not find him. The sergeant and his wife questioned me, and I told both of them that I did not know Alonzo, but Ms. Bessie, the cook, knew that we were best friends. I don't think the sergeant's wife or the sergeant was convinced that I did not know Alonzo. His wife took me home one night, and while I was sitting in the back seat of her car, she asked me again if I knew the boy who came into the restaurant, and I denied it again. While driving on the highway leading to our house, someone was walking along the darkened highway, and I recognized the person as being Alonzo, my friend, who came into the restaurant. The sergeant's wife almost hit him and she said to me, "Oops, I almost hit that little boy." Little did she know that that little boy that she almost hit was the little black boy who integrated in her restaurant. It was very interesting that after that incident, police presence was increased inside the restaurant. That is to say, they frequented the restaurant much more.

    I also tried to be a caddy at the Grand Hotel Golf Course in Point Clear, Alabama, which was the next town over from Fairhope. This was and still is one of the most beautiful golf courses in the country, and people come from all over the country to golf there. Black people could caddy there but could not golf. I remember seeing many of the black teenagers, who were older than me, perfect the game of golf from watching the white men who they caddied for. If black males had been given the opportunity to golf, some of them would have been great golfers. This is another example of how white society stymied the talents and progress of so many people.

    My oldest brother, who loved fishing and caddying, made a great deal of money caddying. I can't remember exactly how caddying worked, but I think he and others were paid $18 for nine holes and $36 for eighteen holes. On many a day, he made $36 or more, and this was good money for a black person, youth or adult, in the 1960s. I tried to caddy once, and the way it worked was that we had to sit in a small room that was about ten feet by twelve feet, and this was called the caddy shack. It was run by a black man whom I was afraid of because I always thought that he was mean and he appeared to me to be an alcoholic. He stood at a blackboard, and he would write people's names on the blackboard, and we would be called to caddy according to needs and requests. I went to the golf course more than once to caddy, but my name was never called and many other teenagers and men were being called. I thought to myself, *I don't like this*. I definitely did not like the idea of sitting around all day, waiting for my name to be called. One day my name was called, and no one had ever told me how to caddy and my concept of a caddy was to merely carry the golf bag. When I walked onto the golf course, I felt a certain level of intensity, and the first thing I did wrong was to step on the green. I remember this white man whom I was supposed to be caddying for looking at me and in a very angry voice and a heavy southern accent, saying to me, "Boy, get the hell off of that green." I didn't know that there were certain areas that you were not supposed to walk on. They sent me back to the caddy shack, and I knew right then that caddying was not for me. Word spread all around the caddy shack and the community about what had happened to me. Instead of the black men, who were seasoned caddies trying to help me, they laughed at me and mocked me. This was something that I never forgot, and this is one reason it is important to be positive role models to kids and build them up, not tear them down. This same golf course is still thriving today, but the main difference is that the golfers use motorized golf carts to carry their golf bags. The golf course is also opened to any person who wants to golf there.

When I was growing up, grown men (black) would caddy on a daily basis to take care of themselves and their families. Even though many of them had graduated from high school, they were locked into jobs that went nowhere. They could never have become a manager of a supermarket, clothing store, police officer, or firefighter because of racism. When the town of Fairhope did decide to hire a black police officer, he could only arrest black people. What happened to the black man and woman in the South in regard to being humiliated, demeaned, and diminished impacted the rest of the country because when blacks fled the South heading north, east, and west, they oftentimes hit a brick wall because again racism and discrimination raised their ugly faces and blacks were trapped in ghettos of every major city in the United States.

I, myself, made that trek as well, and I overcame some very difficult odds. People have asked me on many occasions, "Why did you come to Milwaukee?" I also became very tired of explaining to people that I left Alabama because white people closed all doors of opportunity to blacks in the state of Alabama. Even the governor of Alabama stood in the doorway of the University of Alabama with two Alabama State Troopers to prevent black students from entering. This is a vital part of this nation's history, and everyone needs to know what happened in this country.

When I was a teenager in Alabama, it was not unusual for the Fairhope police to set up a road block. They would stop people and ask to see their driver's license. They always stopped people as they were coming from the black section of town, and it appeared to me that they were only stopping black people. To this day, I still think that they had a hidden agenda in stopping black people.

Our high school principal, Mr. Walker J. Carroll, had a favorite expression, which was, "Strive for excellence." He stood erect and he always carried himself with a great deal of pride, and he expected no less from his students. He was articulate and impeccably dressed in a three-piece suit, every day. Mr. Carroll understood the white southern mentality, and in spite of living in an oppressive society, he encouraged his students to persevere and "strive for excellence." One day he shared with the student body an incident that happened to him at a local bank. He told us that when standing in line in the bank, he was reading the newspaper and a white person in the bank commented, "So they can read." Probably, if he had commented, he could have been arrested for being an "uppity nigger." It was also interesting that black people could stand in the same line with whites in a grocery store, but in the liquor store, there were separate lines, one for whites and one for coloreds.

I also played the snare drum in high school, and every year our band was invited to march and play in the Mardi Gras, which was also held in Mobile, Alabama. The black schools were put at the end of the parade, but we were also the best in what we did. Whenever the black schools would play, you could see the anticipation not just on the faces of black people but on the faces of white people as well.

When I was working at another restaurant in Fairhope, the white bartender commented to me one day that he liked the black bands better than the white bands. He further stated that the black bands were more lively. Our band director was Mr. John Montgomery, a tall, light-skinned, distinguished, and handsome man who could play every instrument in the band, and he was a genius at reading music. He also taught world history, and you got the impression that he was also a genius in this area. He easily taught world history without using a book. Whenever the band would perform at football games or off school grounds, he expected everyone to be on their best behavior. He would always say, "Remember, the white people are watching us."

Mrs. Montgomery was an elementary school teacher, and she always carried a pleasant smile. As I think back on all of the dignified and highly educated black teachers that graduated from places like Fisk, Tuskegee, Spellman, Morehouse, Alabama State, Southern University, and many other outstanding colleges and universities, I become very angry at a society that relegated them to second-class status. They could not even take their families out to a restaurant for a nice seafood dinner or anything. This injustice should not have been tolerated, and this country should be ashamed of itself for sending black men to all of the major wars to die for this country but were never granted freedom at home. How dare the United States try and police the world when she has denied its own citizens basic human rights?

Many of our black children today have no clue of what took place in this country in regard to slavery, racism, oppression, and discrimination. They also feel that they are overworked if they have to make their bed or take the garbage out. In the chapter on my childhood, I have already addressed all of the hard work that was commonplace for many of us. I am very angry that many black kids today take what we went through so lightly. Many of them will say, "I didn't live it, so what?" My parents and grandparents' lives were even more difficult, and they paved the way for me and others, and I am very appreciative. Children and teenagers of today did not experience the sting of racism and discrimination, and because of this, they don't have the same level of determination, perseverance, tenacity, and motivation.

I am proud to say that I am from the South, and I am glad that my parents and my black teachers gave me a solid foundation. Many kids today don't have that foundation, and they don't have a sense of history or who they are. I have had some teenagers say, "I'm glad I wasn't born back then." They don't realize that they've gotten where they are today because of our blood, sweat, and tears. I honor my ancestors for the sacrifices they made, and the teens today should be taught that they're able to go through the front door because we had to go through the back door. It is unfortunate that the generations of many black people today don't know where they're going because they don't know where they came from.

As black kids growing up in Alabama, we had to pass the white high school in our own hometown of Fairhope and go to the next town over to attend an all-black school. This was also the school that my great, great uncle founded, and his picture hung in many of the classrooms and in the auditorium. In high school, I was a very good student, and I always carried a 3.50 grade point average. Upon graduation, I was in the top 10 percent of my graduating class. The teachers expected no less from me, but with the combination of working at the Parker House Restaurant and having a girlfriend, Olivia Harrison, who was a majorette and almost every boy was after, my GPA dropped down to 3.40. High school was the best time of my life, and being in love increased my zeal for life.

Today, I work with many kids who are unmotivated and 50 percent of them are dropping out of school. They also have no idea how this is impacting their future. Many of these youth today are struggling with so many issues, and this causes them to be distracted and school becomes a chore rather than something enjoyable. These years cannot be taken back and to lose them, to me, should be an outrage.

In middle school and high school, I liked reciting poems. My two favorite poems were "If" by Rudyard Kipling and "The Raven" by Edgar Allen Poe. These were my favorite poems to recite, and I also liked "The Creation" by James Weldon Johnson, "Invictus" by Ernest Henley, and an assortment of poems by Langston Hughes.

Mrs. Thelma Carroll, the principal's wife, taught English and she loved poetry. We spent a great deal of time on Shakespeare, and she was articulate, demanding, and passionate about teaching, and she pushed us to our full potential. She was also the music and choir director, and I took choir as an elective. We sang such songs as "Theme from Exodus," "Go Down, Moses," "There Is a Balm in Gilead," and "Sweet Chariot." Mrs. Carroll did not want us to forget from whence we came, and the racial climate in the South and throughout the country was reason enough to continue to sing the slave songs.

As I think back on all of my high school teachers, they were extremely proud people who had gone through many struggles. In spite of these struggles, they always had a smile on their face, and they walked with their head erect and they taught us to do the same. God and religion were part of our school, and every morning before school started, the "Lord's Prayer" was played on the PA system, and everyone sang along in their respective classrooms.

It was during my high school years that I decided that I was going to become Catholic. My father was a minister and an assistant pastor of a Pentecostal Church, and I had a great deal of respect for him. He knew everyone in the community, and everyone knew him and respected him. He was truly a man of God, and almost every adult who knew me thought that I would follow his footsteps. Instead, my oldest brother, Howard, followed his footsteps by becoming a minister, a pastor, and a bishop.

My mother was born gifted with musical talents. She played the piano and the organ excellently and never took music lessons. If she heard a song, she could follow along on the piano or the organ. Whenever she would play the piano or organ, I would play along by tapping on a piece of furniture or other hard item. I guess my musical talents came in the form of drumming. Black churches in the community and outside of the community would pay my mother to play for them. They oftentimes would call her to play for funerals. There were about five or six black churches in the town of Fairhope, and people had a tendency to argue a lot about the Bible and about who was right and who was wrong.

The Catholic church that black people attended was in the next town over, Daphne, where I also attended high school. The Diocese in that area supplied priests and nuns to "evangelize" black Catholics. The name of the Catholic church was Shrine of the Holy Cross, and there was also a school where the nuns taught. The name of the school was also the Shrine of the Holy Cross.

My girlfriend, Olivia, was Catholic, and she also attended the Catholic school through eighth grade. I remember her talking about how mean the nuns were. It appeared to me that the white nuns and priests at the Shrine of the Holy Cross may have been the only white people who showed a true interest in educating black children from a religious and academic standpoint. Olivia talked about all of the Holy Days of Obligation, and on these days it appeared to me that the Catholic church expected every practicing Catholic to attend mass on these days.

Olivia, I remember, was quite serious about her religion, and she put aside everything else to attend mass on Sunday and holy days. Whenever I would do something or say something that she thought was sinful, she would remind me of the meaning of venial sins (small sins) and mortal sins. I was not completely convinced of this notion nor was I convinced that there was a limbo or a purgatory. You could not argue with Olivia on these issues because she was a true believer. I admired her for her commitment and dedication to Catholicism. There was also a larger white Catholic church in the city of Daphne, and one Sunday, Olivia decided to attend the white church (Christ the King), and after mass a white male parishioner followed her out of the church and told her to go to her own church. This one experience altered her belief system, and I think she started to question her own faith.

My parents, I think, were a little shaken that I chose Catholicism because I don't think that they liked the way Catholics worshipped. They would always make comments about praying to Mary, worshipping idol gods, and they definitely did not like the idea of playing bingo. I started attending CCD classes (Confraternity of Christian Doctrines) in the Catholic church and I liked the classes, and Catholicism seemed right for me. After CCD classes, it was customary to have dances on Friday nights, and I loved the dances.

In the Pentecostal religion, they frowned on dancing or gambling of any kind. For me, I felt like I had to walk around feeling guilty all the time because everything was a sin. I didn't feel these constraints in the Catholic church, and I started attending mass at the Shrine of the Holy Cross. My mother and father were not happy, but I was convicted in what I wanted to do. I was the only one in the family who converted to Catholicism, but I guess I was also the only one who did a lot of things differently. Pentecostals are much more animated, and back then I was afraid of *tarrying* and "getting the Holy Ghost." I saw church members getting the Holy Ghost, and sometimes they would lie out in the middle of the floor and their body would gyrate as if they were having a seizure. They would speak in tongues, and as a small boy and a teenager, I didn't want to open myself up to the Holy Ghost, which came upon people suddenly. I wanted to be in complete control, and if I was speaking in tongues, I wasn't in control.

As a devout practicing Catholic today, I truly believe in the Holy Spirit, which my parents called the Holy Ghost. I did not understand speaking in tongues, but I believe that in all faiths and all religions, we all have the capacity to speak in tongues. I believe that this ability is innate and somehow primitive or primordial. To put it another way, this ability may have been part of our repertoire when the first breath of life was blown into human kind.

When I attended CCD classes and mass at Shrine of the Holy Cross as a teenager, the priest's name was Father Brown. Father Brown was white, and he was well-known, and he seemed like he loved everybody. He took a liking to me, and he always encouraged higher education. Whenever we had our Friday night dances after CCD classes, he would always walk through the dance hall and greet everyone.

One time we were coming from a family reunion, and Olivia's brother-in-law was stopped by an Alabama State Trooper. He wasn't speeding or anything because I was driving behind him. When the trooper pulled him over, I inquired about why he was being pulled over. The trooper immediately turned on me and told me to tend to my own business. I then asked him what grounds he had to arrest him, and at that point he knocked a sandwich out of my hand that I was holding. I was then thrown into the back of his car and taken to the Fairhope Police Station and jailed.

In route to the station he called in to the dispatcher and stated, "I'm bringing in a smart black nigger." He went on to tell me, "Nigger, we ought to take you to Bay Minette instead and keep you there." Bay Minette was the county seat, and they had a larger jail. If a person went to the Bay Minette jail, there was a good chance that they would be sitting there for a while. It was a well-known fact that black people did not want to go to jail in Bay Minette because the white judges had a reputation for not being fair. If a black person worked for a well-known white person and they went before a judge, the judge was more lenient because the black person's boss pulled some strings.

The state trooper did take me to the Fairhope jail, and they put me in a cell with another older black male who was a habitual thief. The cell was about eight feet wide and eight feet long. The other person in the cell seemed very relaxed and unafraid. I admit that I was afraid because I was unsure of my fate. I guess it was a policy that you could make one phone call. They did come in and ask me who I wanted to call. I initially was going to say that I wanted to call my father, but I didn't want him to know what had happened. I instinctively stated, "I'd like to call Father Brown." When I said this, the white officer gave me a strange look. They knew that Father Brown was a powerful man, and I got the feeling that they did not want to play around with a man of God. Within twenty minutes of them asking me who I wanted to call, they released me and I wasn't charged with anything. Father Brown knew my character, and he may have even called the police station. They could have taken me to the Bay Minette (County) jail, which was about thirty-five miles away, and they could have roughed me up on the back roads along the way. Instead, the Holy Spirit came into that cell that day. Even though my father did not know what was going on, he was a praying man and I'm sure at that moment, he felt my distress.

As high school students, there was no such thing as not working. Most of the boys had jobs at places like country clubs, restaurants, farms, or doing lawn work. Also, everyone was slim and trim with very little body fat. In fact, we used to have arm wrestling contests all the time, and we used to boast about whose biceps were bigger. Many of the kids today are obese and out of shape, and the unfortunate thing is that their parents may outlive them due to inactive lifestyles.

I also prided myself on public speaking while in high school, and I had the good fortune of winning two interstate second-place trophies in public speaking. The girls took economics, and many of the boys took agriculture. I'm not sure why I took agriculture, but maybe the leaders of the state of Alabama thought that we were all going to be farmers. It was interesting that a distinction was made between white students and black students. Black students were called New Farmers of America, and the white students were called the Future Farmers of America.

Many people may wonder still today why we have such organizations like the Association of Black Psychologists, Black Teacher's Association, or the Black Police Union. Whites deliberately kept us out of organizations, so black people started and maintained their own organizations. Many white people in the South were content as long as black people did not buck the system or rock the boat. As I was growing up in Alabama, the people were either black or Caucasian. You did not see many people of other backgrounds other than Mexicans, and they worked the fields. As a young boy, I worked side by side with Mexicans in the hot sun in Irish potato fields. Instead of Irish potatoes, we used to call them *lish* potatoes because we didn't know any better, and that's how the adults pronounced it. This also reinforces the fact that our environment is critical in our development. When kids go to school and say "Yo mama" instead of your mother, or "I be having a good time" instead of "I'm having a good time," they're merely mimicking what they hear and assume to be correct.

As I think back on my early years growing up in rural Alabama, I came to the realization that black men were rendered impotent from the standpoint of not being able to vote, being diminished to childlike status, and being degraded and humiliated in front of their family. Other than being a teacher or an insurance salesman for a black insurance company, black males did not hold other professional jobs. The black insurance companies also exploited black people. If black people paid into a life insurance policy for fifty or sixty years, they were lucky if the policy paid five thousand dollars for burial. Men in the community usually were common laborers, mechanics, cooks, barbers, chauffeurs, waiters, or they worked on a farm.

The Grand Hotel Marriott, which used to be just the Grand Hotel, in Point Clear, Alabama, hired most of the black people of

Fairhope, Point Clear, and surrounding areas as cooks, housekeepers, chauffeurs, yard keepers, and maître d's. In high school, I was also a substitute bus driver, and I was one of the few students who the regular bus driver trusted to fill in for him. I loved driving and it was a good feeling to be able to impress and safely transport a busload of my peers. Some nights I even picked band members up for football games.

I never thought twice about leaving Oak Creek, Wisconsin, and returning to attend high school in Alabama. I was where I wanted to be, and it was rewarding for me to attend an all-black high school in Alabama, where dignity, pride, and respect took precedence.

I enjoyed and gained a lot from my multicultural experience in Oak Creek, Wisconsin, but that chapter of my life was closed and I needed to move on.

The white kids in Alabama did not know us, and we did not know them. We all missed out on a lot because of this disconnect and the stupidity and ignorance of governmental officials in power. Segregation prevented black students and white students from being lifetime friends, and having the opportunity to mingle was never an option.

As was stated earlier, my high school years were the best years of my life. One day a teacher who did not teach me came up to me and said to me, "So you're Earl Bracy. I don't know what all of the girls are going crazy about, you're nothing special."

Our vice principal, Mr. Taylor, was impeccably dressed. He also spent a great deal of time patrolling the campus, and he had a great deal of wisdom and he had a sixth sense for detecting campus conflicts. One day the gym teacher's daughters (twins) asked me for some change, and I reached into my pocket and gave both of them money. They were sixth or seventh graders, and the elementary school was next door. They also probably felt comfortable asking me for money because I considered their sister, who was in high school, to be my girlfriend, and of course this was before I was involved with Olivia. When Mr. Taylor saw me give them change from my pocket, he made them give it back to me, and he gave me a stern lecture in why I should not have been giving them money. His words were, "If they're asking you for money now, they will expect men to give them money." The words that he imparted to me stuck with me, and I'm sure his words stuck with the twins as well.

My boxing gloves followed me from Oak Creek, Wisconsin, to Fairhope, Alabama. I loved boxing, but I also discovered that even though I made my mark, the black kids were harder to beat than the white kids in Oak Creek, Wisconsin. Some of the black kids that I boxed in Alabama had some very good raw talent, and I was dropped to my knees a couple of times. Also, in the South, the schools are big in basketball and football. Swimming, wrestling, and soccer were basically nonexistent.

Our school was on Highway 98, which was a scenic route along Mobile Bay, and traffic was always heavy because of tourism. As I think back on my high school years, I don't think that I would have wanted to live in any other area. Fairhope and Daphne were, and still are, beautiful, historic, quaint, and picturesque. I did not fully understand the richness of this area until I moved away. Daphne, itself, was called the Jubilee City. As explained earlier, a jubilee occurs when fresh water and salt water come together in Mobile Bay, and all types of fish, shrimp, and crabs become dazed and they come ashore, and the local citizenry scoop them up with nets and spears. As far as I know, the seafood is and was safe to consume.

Native to this area are oak trees (with moss) that are over two hundred years old, majestic pine trees, azaleas, and the weather can be extremely hot.

Another good thing about my high school years is that there was never a homicide of any student, although homicides did occur. There was never a fatal automobile accident that I recall, and we respected and listened to adults. Spirituality was also extremely important, and church property was definitely holy ground. In spite of segregation, discrimination, oppression, racial hatred, and marginality, we all had a great deal of pride and people smiled a lot more than we do today.

Our high school principal reported getting calls from the mayor of the town of Fairhope, telling him that the black students were too loud on the bus as we came through the downtown section of Fairhope. Many times I personally felt that it was unfounded when the principal reminded all of us to maintain respect, pride, and dignity because, "Whether you like it or not, the white people are watching you."

In high school, I was always thinking of ways to make money. A lady in the neighborhood, Mrs. Ethel Hall, who operated a small restaurant and was a very good cook, asked me to take slices of her potato pies and chocolate candy to school to sell. She gave me a portion of the money that was made, and I also worked a few hours in her restaurant. In a sense, things came easy for me because peers and adults liked me.

On another note, I am sure that many people have no idea how pecans are harvested. My father had many jobs, and one of his jobs was contracting to harvest the pecans from the white farmers' orchards. Many of the pecans would fall from the trees, and the others had to be shaken from the trees. My father would climb the trees and shake the branches or use a fishing pole to dislodge the pecans.

One year while in high school, I remember going to the pecan field by myself and picking up pecans for extra money. The farmers usually paid us three to five cents a pound. Once they were picked, we poured them into a croker sack and took them to the farmer's shed, where he weighed them. If he paid us five cents a pound, he would collect around one dollar or more per pound when he sold them to a distributor. On this particular evening, when I decided to pick pecans until dark, it was February 13. That evening, I think I picked over a hundred pounds, and I went to what was called a five and dime store and bought the biggest box of candy that was heart-shaped for my Valentine for the next day. It was hard work, but I remember getting great satisfaction out of doing this. I was also teased for buying such a big box of candy.

As I stated earlier, my high school years were the best years of my life. Many kids today are unmotivated, apathetic, and misguided. They are living in somewhat of a twilight zone, and many will have no high school memories to cherish. When I graduated from high school, I was attached to my teachers. After receiving my diploma, I felt that someone had pulled the rug from underneath me. The change process was hard, but I was stepping out into the real world.

All through high school, my teachers talked about the future, and finally, here it was, staring me right in the face.

After graduating from high school, the same day that I left Alabama coming to Wisconsin, a white army recruiter was headed to our house. Our paths crossed for the last time, and his final statement to me was, "If we don't get you now, we will get you later." At that time, it was just so interesting to me that black soldiers were being killed in Vietnam in the name of freedom and democracy, but they could not be buried in "white" cemeteries in the South, and this was true in Fairhope, Alabama.

The all black high school in Daphne, Alabama

Rev. S. B. Bracy, my great-great uncle and founder of Baldwin County Training School

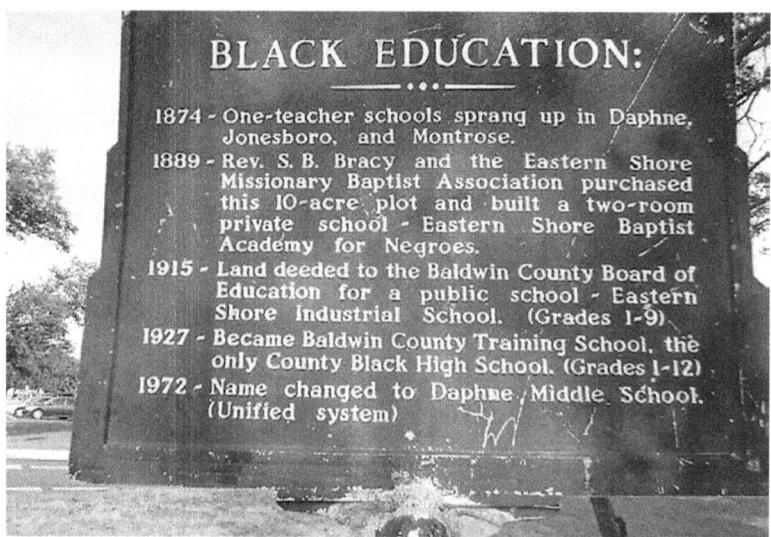

Black Education: 1889 Reverend S. B. Bracy and the Eastern Shore Missionary Baptist Association purchased a ten-acre plot and built a two-room private school, Eastern Shore Baptist Academy for Negroes.

The Grand Hotel Golf Course in Point Clear,
Alabama, where I attempted to caddy

Mr. Walker J. Carroll, principal of Baldwin County Training School

The first school that my great, great uncle founded is now the Black Education Museum.

The Shrine of the Holy Cross Catholic Church

Christ the King Catholic Church

Bethlehem Temple Church that my father
copastored and at times pastored

Twin Beech AME Zion Church

A picture of the old jail cell in Fairhope, Alabama, where I was taken

Mr. Lemuel Taylor, vice principal of Baldwin County Training School

This black church sits along Highway 98 near Mobile Bay and the old high school. It is also as old as the majestic pine and oak trees that surround it.

This is the new Fairhope High School that today is totally integrated and racial harmony exists.

CHAPTER FOUR

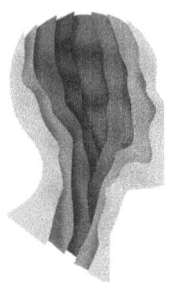

My Northern Migration to Milwaukee

After graduating from high school, I decided to return back to Milwaukee. My uncle, Wilmer Matherson, with whom I lived in Oak Creek, Wisconsin, was determined for me to return back to Wisconsin. The same year that I graduated from high school, he sold his home in Oak Creek and moved to a flat in Milwaukee. I was shocked to discover that he and my aunt had separated. My uncle was anxious for me to leave the state of Alabama because he visited there during my high school years, and he did not like the fact that black people were marginalized to the degree that they could not sit down and order a meal at any restaurant. With any restaurant chain, black people could order from the back door, but they could not sit down in the main dining room and enjoy a meal.

My trip to Milwaukee from Alabama was on a Greyhound bus and I remember thinking about my decision. I was slightly conflicted but there was a strong force pulling me towards Milwaukee. The night before I left Alabama, I spent a great deal of time with my high school sweetheart, Olivia Harrison, who later became my wife. I'm sure she must have felt abandoned, especially since we had spent so much time together in high school and we were considered as being one of the most popular couples.

Settling into the Milwaukee area after high school was a little difficult for me from the standpoint that I was experiencing some anxiety and possible mild depression from being separated from my girlfriend of four years. We didn't have e-mail, cell phones, or texting then, and letters from her seemed to have taken forever to come. Whenever I did not receive a letter as expected, my spirits would spiral downward. It was also quite interesting living with my uncle. He was pro education and he meant well. He made sure that I was involved in the YMCA and he would always check to see if I was around positive peers. Living with him was a little stressful because my life was not my life, and even though he meant well, he had a controlling spirit and his assessment of what I was doing with my free time was inaccurate. Since I was away from my parents, I'm sure he felt that he was responsible for me. He drove me all over the city looking for jobs, and on other occasions, I'd take the city bus. Milwaukee is an interesting city in many ways. Firstly, it seems to be always cloudy and cool. Because of Lake Michigan, the weather can drop to forty degrees in a matter of minutes. The city also had an interesting and peculiar smell for various reasons. In the downtown area, the odors from the breweries, Ambrosia Chocolate Company, Wonder Bread, which was a bakery, the Tannery, and sometimes the slaughterhouse would all blend in together, and this was Milwaukee's trademark. Sometimes one smell would be more pronounced depending on wind direction and velocity.

In the late 1960s, Milwaukee was an interesting city from another standpoint. There was so much racial polarization, discrimination, racial prejudice, containment of black people, redlining, white flight, and xenophobia from the standpoint that many white Milwaukeeans saw black people as a threat. There were rigid boundaries put in place in regard to where black people could and could not live. The interesting thing was that in spite of white hostility, the opportunities in spite of racial discrimination were much better for black people in Milwaukee than they were for many black people in Alabama, or any southern state for that matter. Black people left the South for the North because even if they were qualified for a job in the South, in many instances, they would not be hired.

Upon arriving in Milwaukee after high school, I worked at many different jobs. My first job was with a janitorial company, which was called Ace Janitorial Service. We cleaned windows and large department stores after they closed at night. Many times we worked until 3:00 a.m. I remember one night, the person in charge was leaving a store that we had just finished cleaning. He was white, and the rest of the people in the car were all white. I was sitting in the back seat, and a white female was sitting next to me. When the driver stopped for a light, I happened to have looked behind me through the rear window, and two white police officers in a squad car were behind us. When the light turned green, they followed us and subsequently put their red lights and sirens on. The driver got out of the car and showed them his identification, and they wanted to know what our business was. I'm sure the only reason they stopped him was because they wanted to know who I was. They saw a black male sitting in the back seat next to a white female, and they wanted to find out what I was up to. This was all too common in Milwaukee at that time. Policemen did not need an excuse to stop and detain black males. We were not afforded respect and dignity. As far as many police officers were concerned, black males were guilty until proven innocent. When you have to live with this type of humiliation on a daily basis, your psyche is affected and your self-worth is diminished.

My second job after high school was with the Milwaukee County Mental Health Complex as a psychiatric aide. This may have also been when I became interested in psychology. It was also here that I learned that mental illness has no bias. It affects people of all backgrounds and nationalities, and working at the complex was a humbling experience for me. It reinforced the fact that no one should demean or humiliate another human being because of their race or nationality. Working as a psychiatric aide, my job was to take temperatures, vitals, bathe, housekeeping, helping patients to get dressed, grooming, such as shaving, playing cards with some patients, taking them to church, feeding the ones who needed help, and listening. There were also prominent people who were patients. Some suffered from schizophrenia, depression, and some simply had a nervous breakdown.

One incident that stands out in my mind was when a man in his thirties feigned mental illness because of a crime that he had committed. His intent was that he wanted to be committed to a mental hospital rather than go to prison. One day he was sitting in the day room, and he had a metal spoon in his hand that he kept after eating his breakfast. I was not sure what he was going to do with the spoon, and as I watched him, he slightly bent the spoon and what he was doing was bending it to the curvature of his esophagus. After doing this, he looked at the spoon and swallowed it. The spoon was approximately six to seven inches long.

After swallowing the spoon, he refused to have a bowel movement for several days. Consequently, X-rays were taken, and he was seen by a team of psychologists and psychiatrists and deemed to have been sane, and he was transported to a state prison in handcuffs and shackles. There were many occasions when I worked a double shift, and I would have to take two different buses to get home. The first bus would take me from the Mental Health Complex (Milwaukee County Hospital) to downtown Milwaukee. When I worked a double shift, I would oftentimes have to wait at the downtown bus stop for several minutes before transferring to the second bus. While waiting for the bus at 1:00 a.m., what was shocking to me was that there were a lot of white men who cruised the downtown area in big fancy cars looking for males to pick up. These cars would pull up to the bus stop, back to back, as if they were a taxi cab. Being a naive kid from Alabama, I had to get used to city life, and this was definitely a culture shock for me. I told my uncle about my experiences, and he knew right away what the men were up to. His reaction is forever etched in my memory. When I mentioned it to him, his response was, "*Don't you ever go up to their cars. They're fags.*"

I guess the word *fag* was en vogue at that time.

I also bagged groceries and did stocking at a grocery store called Galst Food Market on Sixteenth Street and North Avenue in Milwaukee on Fridays and Saturdays. The store was always packed. On the first of each month, many women received their welfare check and some type of food allowance, and the store would be wall-to-wall people. Many people were poor, but unlike today, they always had a smile on their face, and even though life was hard for many, there was a lot less anger than we see today. Galst Food Market was a place where people shopped for collard greens, turnip greens, chitlins, and other southern foods. Mr. Galst, who owned the store, helped many people in the community, and everyone knew him as Julie. He was Jewish, and during the riots of 1967, his store was untouched. That shows the level of respect that everyone in the community had for him. It's also interesting that many of the teenagers who worked in his store went on to college, and some are doctors, lawyers, and other professions. As an employer, he also planted positive seeds of encouragement.

As a nineteen-year-old, I was also hired as a fork lift driver at A. O. Smith Corporation. A. O. Smith manufactured car frames and other parts that were sent out to General Motors and other companies. Many black males in the black community were hired by A. O. Smith, and A. O. Smith was a fortress in the community. They paid a very good salary to their workers, and they provided excellent medical benefits. Many black people came here from the South looking for the Promised Land, and they found it in A. O. Smith. When A. O. Smith went out of business in the 1990s, this devastated the black community.

Another very good job that I had was at Continental Can Company, working as a press operator. My responsibility was to remove tops for beer and soda cans as they came through the press. The work environment was noisy but somewhat friendly. I remember only one or two other black people working there. A friend of mine who was black applied for a position with me, but I was hired and he wasn't. We were given a test that I passed, but he didn't. I felt bad for him for a long time because he was good at many things. He probably could have repaired the machines when they broke down. He repaired his own cars and he was very good with his hands, and I felt that he could have worked circles around me at my job. I believe that this was an example of a quota system. I don't think it would have mattered what my friend scored on his test. Their intent was to only hire one of us. At some places of employment in Milwaukee, that was the mind-set when it came to being fair to blacks.

During the riots of 1967, a city emergency was declared because of the widespread looting and the damage done in the city of Milwaukee. The National Guard was called in, and businesses had to be closed because no one was moving. During the riots, and more specifically, during the quarantine, National Guardsmen stood at almost every corner on the north side of Milwaukee. I was unaware of the state of emergency issued by the governor and attempted to drive to work. First, I walked two blocks down to ask a National Guardsman if it was OK to drive to work. He was a young white guardsman, and as I got closer to him, he walked up to me and told me to halt, but before doing that, he placed the barrel of his rifle against my chest. I politely told him where I worked and asked if it was OK to drive. He stated that there was a state of emergency and ordered me to return to my home. I thanked him and left, but afterward, I realized how easily I could have been shot. When I was allowed to return back to work, everyone, including the foreman, looked at me with suspicion as if I was the cause of the riots because I was black. There were unspoken words, but I felt that many of them felt that I had to have been an active participant in the destruction that was brought to the city. The foreman assigned everybody a press and overlooked me, and I'm sure it was done purposely. A white female employee reminded him that I didn't have a press to operate. He had no reaction other than to say, "OK, I forgot you?" The press he assigned me was at the very back of the plant, and it was breaking down about every ten minutes. Each time it broke down, the mechanic had to come over and repair it, and during this day he didn't present with his usual smile. In fact, it was quite a while before normalcy set in again. It's not a good feeling to be condemned for something you had no part in.

I remember vividly the night the riots started. That night, a friend and I were double-dating, and we had taken our dates to an outdoor movie theater (the 41 Twin). I drove my car that night, and without saying, there were no cell phones but there was a strange occurrence. There were back-to-back announcements that came over the PA system telling people to call home immediately. It looked as if it was going to rain that night, and we assumed that a storm was coming. Being teenagers, we were not fazed by inclement weather. After a while, over half of the cars at the theater had started to leave, and it did start to rain. As we drove back to the city and the closer we got to the north side of Milwaukee, where most of the black people lived, we started to see a plethora of police cars, marked and unmarked, with their red lights on and sirens blasting, coming from all directions. The closer we got to the city, the harder the rain came down. People were leaving the theater because the riots had started, and the rain could have been divine intervention because I truly believe that if it had not rained, the looting would have been worse, the death toll higher, and the damage to the city, more severe. When I dropped my date off, the rain was coming down so hard until I could barely see the highway. As I headed toward my apartment, I had to travel down what is now known as Martin Luther King Drive. As I looked out of my car window, I could see brand-new cars overturned on a well-known car lot in the city. There had been reports of sniper fire throughout the night, and if the severe rain had not fallen, I shudder to think about what could have happened. There were multiple fires throughout the city, and if the rain wasn't coming down as heavy as it was, I could have been in a crossfire or I could have been stopped by an already spooked police department and charged with a crime that I had no part in. My parents taught me how to be respectful and law-abiding, and this is something that I always carried with me. The year 1967 was a year of racial tension across the nation, and riots broke out in many major cities. Milwaukee was highly segregated by race, and ethnicity and fair housing legislation was critically needed.

Being born and raised in Alabama, I witnessed discrimination firsthand. However, while in Alabama, I never saw a Ku Klux Klan member dressed in a robe and hood. Shockingly, I saw my first KKK member dressed in his full garb in Wauwatosa, Wisconsin, at an open housing march. Because my psyche was negatively affected by racism and second-class citizenship that I withstood in Alabama, I decided to join the NAACP Youth Council, and I participated in the open housing marches with Father James Groppi. I was young, fearless, and decided to take up a cause, and my convictions were strong. Most of the open housing marches were televised, and we always had to confront angry white crowds who chanted many racial epithets such as "Niggers, go back to Africa," "Monkeys," and "Stay in your own neighborhood." We had cherry bombs thrown at us and sometimes bricks, bottles and other objects, in spite of heavy police protection. We were always reminded to not break ranks, and Father Groppi was a lightning rod. In retrospect, he may have also had his own agenda, and as he marched us into battle, it could have been our last battle but everyone saw him as a savior.

At this time, I was still living with my uncle, and he must have seen the marches on TV because they were headline news every day. I was also taking college classes at Milwaukee Area Technical College, which was then Milwaukee Institute of Technology, and I was probably starting to individuate and question injustice and unjust laws. My uncle came to me, and he said, "I'm going to have to send you back to Alabama." He knew that marching on the south side of Milwaukee with Father Groppi was dangerous, not only from the standpoint of confronting a hostile white crowd, but also a hostile white police force. I understood my uncle's concerns, but I informed him that I was going to be moving to a rooming house, which I did. The rooming house was on First Street and Center, and it is still standing today. There were approximately eight to ten bedrooms with a bathroom upstairs and one downstairs. There was one main kitchen that all of the men shared, and we had to wait our turn to take a shower. My uncle seemed hurt that I was leaving, but I felt that I was also entering manhood and I needed my independence and autonomy. One of his friends begged and pleaded for me not to leave him, but my decision was made. I also appreciated the fact that my uncle came by regularly to check on me. Likewise, I also visited him.

At that time, I did not realize that my uncle was only trying to protect me. I could have been easily killed by a police officer or a jeering white mob on the south side of Milwaukee. At that time, you did not find black people on the south side of Milwaukee unless they worked there. This was because of the level of racial hatred and disdain that whites had for blacks. Even though there was a strong police and National Guard presence, my uncle still had grave concerns about my safety. It is very interesting that when you are a teenager, you don't always think about safety.

The man who owned the rooming house was German, and one day he offered to put me in a better room at a different location if I would shovel snow off the sidewalk and steps. The sidewalk was almost a block long, so he must have owned almost all of the buildings on the block. When he relocated me to the next rooming house, it was a step down instead of a step up. The room was half the size of my old room, and there was barely enough room to put a television. I felt exploited and used, and I think many people saw black people as being stupid and naive.

The men at this rooming house took me under their wings since I was the youngest one there. They all worked full-time jobs, and they were either divorced or their wives had put them out. It was interesting that they would start partying at about 5:00 p.m. on Fridays, and late Sunday evening, they would start toning down and getting ready for work on Monday. They all had a tendency to brag about the women in their lives.

My room was on the second floor and adjacent to a funeral home. From my bedroom window, I could look down into the dining area of the funeral home. Having a curious mind, I oftentimes wondered what took place inside the funeral home. During this time period, I was still a member of the NAACP Youth Council and still marching with Father Groppi. I soon discovered that whenever I parked my car in front of the NAACP headquarters, the detectives would follow me all the way to the rooming house. They never stopped me, but I was followed quite a bit. I never had a police record, so I guess they saw no need to harass me. However, today, I'm sure my name is somewhere in their files for merely exercising my rights as an American and standing up for justice.

I also looked for other places to live in Milwaukee, and I responded to an ad and looked at a place above a tavern on Walnut Street. The landlord was white, and he agreed to meet me at the rental property. When we walked upstairs into the room, I could not believe my eyes. The dust was about an inch thick, the carpet was molded, and rat pellets covered the entire floor as well as the kitchen sink. I could not believe that this man was showing me filth. Again, it showed me that his perception of black people was that we're stupid and we'll live in squalor and filth. Humaneness must be practiced at all times. Humankind's inhumanity to one another is what will destroy us if we're not watchful.

During this same time period, before I started working, someone told me that the School of Dentistry at Marquette University would do dental work free because the dental students would be doing it. I remember taking a bus to Marquette and waiting in the waiting area to be seen. When my name was called, the receptionist took my slip and stated that there would be a fifty-cent charge. At that time, I had no money on me. She then took my slip, ripped it up, threw it in the garbage, and said, "We can't help you." It was an experience that I never forgot, and wherever that lady is today, I'm sure it came back to her in some form or fashion. The moral of the story is always be compassionate, understanding, respectful, and humble toward your fellow human beings.

Living in Milwaukee during the late 1960s, you always got the feeling that it was about containment and control. The police department's agenda was to contain and control. There were many times in Milwaukee when I was stopped by the police for simply walking at night. I would be coming from work, and their two favorite questions to ask were, "Where are you coming from?" and "Where are you going?" I truly believe that the order of the day was to see how many black men they could strip off their dignity and humiliate.

During this period, we were at the height of the Vietnam War, and Uncle Sam had other plans for me. I abruptly left Milwaukee because I was drafted by the army. After serving three years in the army, I returned back to Milwaukee in 1971.

During the riots in Milwaukee in 1967, these black women were stopped and searched while on their way to work. One of them was also a registered nurse.

An angry white mob confronted us when we marched on the south side of Milwaukee.

THE MAKING OF A BLACK PSYCHOLOGIST

I marched with Father James Groppi for open housing in Milwaukee in 1967. Father Groppi is directly behind me, and I am holding the flag off to the right.

The NAACP Youth Council Freedom House was teargassed by the Milwaukee Police Department, and it was destroyed because of the ensuing fire.

We gathered in front of the Freedom House when the fire was extinguished.

An open housing rally in Milwaukee

Confronted by counter-demonstrators during an open housing march

While living in Alabama, I never saw a KKK member in full garb. My first exposure was at a counter demonstration by KKK members in Wauwatosa, Wisconsin, in 1967.

The rooming house where I lived on First and Center Street in Milwaukee

The second rooming house where I lived was on First and North Avenue next door to a funeral home. Milwaukee detectives followed me home quite frequently but never stopped me.

CHAPTER FIVE

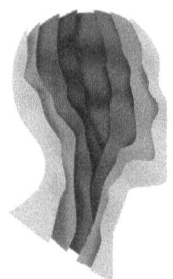

My Army Experience during the Vietnam War

When I was in middle school in Oak Creek, Wisconsin, we used to watch the Army National Guardsmen train with a great deal of tenacity. The National Guard unit was about 150 yards from the school. One day while in an English class, our English teacher took time to give us a history lesson in warfare and military might. "Those reservists out there," he explained, "are not training just to be training. They're getting ready to be shipped off to the Republic of Vietnam." I did not understand fully what he was saying at the time, but I got the message later.

When I was in high school in Alabama, an army recruiter came to the school on several occasions to mainly see if he could recruit males. The males in my class either went on to college or the military via the draft. The army recruiter was white, and this was an all-black school. He was more interested in filling a quota than anything else. This recruiter also used trickery on me and several other students by having us go to Montgomery, Alabama's Maxwell Air Force Base to "take a few aptitude tests." What he did not tell us was that we would be spending the night, and in addition to taking aptitude tests, we would also be taking an army physical. This is one time that I didn't think we'd be coming back home, even though we hadn't graduated from high school. When we did return home, the recruiter made multiple visits to my parent's home, and he also called on multiple occasions but could never reach me. His final words to me were, "If we don't get you now, we'll get you later." I never forgot those words because they came true.

I left Alabama en route to Milwaukee after graduation from high school, and I was drafted into the army two years later. There was a swearing-in ceremony at the reception station in Milwaukee, and after the preliminaries were done, we were supposed to fly into Louisville, Kentucky, and take a bus to Fort Campbell, Kentucky, for basic training. This was my first time flying, so I did not know what to expect. I remember the plane shaking a lot, and there was a loud popping sound while at about 25,000 feet. Instead of landing in Louisville, we made an emergency landing in St. Louis, and we were put on another plane. While on the first plane, none of us was aware of any problem.

When we arrived at Fort Campbell, I wasn't sure what to expect. A driver picked us up in a large OD green army bus and transported us to what I thought was our company. It was the middle of July, and the temperature at Fort Campbell was in the high nineties. As we exited the comfortable, air-conditioned bus with our thirty-pound duffel bags, we were met by drill sergeants and they were not smiling. After a while, our smiles disappeared, and we were about to enter a whole new world (a mean world that none of us understood.) The drill sergeants immediately started giving orders, and if there was such a thing as human dignity and respect, ours had been stripped in a matter of minutes. I think that the bus driver parked the bus about a mile from our platoon, and we had to double time (run) to the barracks with the duffel bag on our shoulder. Many of my comrades were crying, sweating profusely, falling, refusing to get up, and screaming out in agony. The drill sergeants were cursing us out and calling us names such as punks, fags, cunts, and girls. Some of the guys would lie on the ground, and the drill sergeant would tell us to step on them if they fall in front of us. I made it up in my mind that I would not be broken. I was proud of my physique and my stamina. I grew up in Alabama where hard work was the order of the day, and running with a duffel bag that weighed thirty pounds didn't faze me too much. I did get tired, but I ran the mile with the thirty-pound duffel bag. Many of the other trainees were not accustomed to hard work, and many of them had to literally crawl to the finish line.

After arriving at the barracks, we all hoped that we would not be singled out by the drill sergeants. They picked on two people in particular. One was tall and had a great deal of strength, and the other one was weak and he became the scapegoat. The stronger one became the platoon leader, and the weaker one was humiliated and demeaned throughout basic training. On the first day, we all watched him be humiliated, demeaned, and dehumanized in amazement, disbelief, and horror. We were also helpless to do anything about it. The drill sergeants made him crawl in the mud like a pig, and he was screaming like a pig. After crawling in the mud repeatedly, they would then wet him down with a hose, and the water was very cold. While they were hosing him down, they were also calling him derogatory names. Many days this trainee would be, at the instructions of the drill sergeants, running around the barracks with his rifle on top of his head, saying over and over again, until he was told to stop, "I am a shitbird." No one in the platoon was exempt from this humiliation, and it definitely did not enhance one's self-esteem. I remember writing a letter home to my mother hoping to garner some sympathy because we had to get up at 4:30 a.m. every morning. I remember her writing me back and not having much sympathy. Her reply was, "Well, the other boys have to do it too." What she was telling me was to deal with it. Many times after coming back to the barracks from training all day, it was not unusual to find your mattress on the floor. The barracks were inspected every day, and if the bed was made incorrectly and the blanket was not snug enough, everything was thrown on the floor. There were also days when it was too hot to train, and they would suspend all training due to temperatures that were ninety-three degrees or higher. The heat did not bother me due to the fact that I was born in Alabama and oftentimes worked in ninety-five-degree temperatures without taking many breaks for water or anything else.

Before breakfast every morning, we ran for five miles, and after a while, five miles seemed very minuscule. We were usually loaded with combat gear, and this made it tougher but manageable. For some reason, the army put a great deal of emphasis on low crawling, and we spent a great deal of time low crawling, which was probably useful in Vietnam.

Bivouac, which was part of our training as well, meant that we marched (double-timed) to a remote area of Fort Campbell, Kentucky, and set up tents, and this was our home for a few days and nights. Because I was on KP (kitchen police) duty, I was not able to march out to the bivouac area with the rest of the troops. We were brought out on a pickup truck, and we were told by the mess sergeant that we would be able to pitch our tents once we got there. However, after arriving around midnight, we started hammering stakes into the ground to assemble our tents, and within about forty seconds of our banging, a sergeant yelled out, "Shut up that got damn noise and go to bed." The promises that were made to us were not kept, and I ended up sleeping in a sleeping blanket that was extremely cold. Two of my toes were extremely cold, and they felt numb for several months. I'm sure it was frostbite.

As part of our training, we also had to pull guard duty. The army would take us out to a remote area of the woods and leave us out there, one soldier at a time. I was dropped off in the middle of nowhere on military land and left there with an M14 rifle and no ammunition. This was a scary and eerie feeling because I'd hear all kinds of sounds but you never saw anything move. As night fell, it became even more scary because you knew that you were in the middle of nowhere with an unloaded rifle. Finally, after being spooked on multiple occasions, I saw a set of headlights approaching from a distance. I was hoping that it was a military vehicle coming to pick me up. I then thought to myself, *What if it isn't?*

The vehicle approached me, and I could then see the green army color. The driver then stated, "State your name, rank, and serial number." In an actual combat situation, this is what was expected of us.

The only time that the drill sergeants were nice to us was when we went to the rifle range where we were able to fire off hundreds of rounds of live ammunition. We also had to throw live hand grenades, and this also kept the drill sergeants on their toes. I never experienced any knee problems until going in the military, and I think that I was fitted with oversized combat boots that caused my problems. After going on sick call, I was given Darvocet-N, but the drill sergeants still thought I was malingering.

Fort Campbell was also the home of the 101st Airborne Division, and members had a tremendous amount of pride, arrogance, tenacity, fearlessness, and esprit de corps. There also seemed to have been a great deal of tension between the paratroopers, and the MPs (military police) were always there to break up fights, especially on weekends.

The drill sergeants had this thing about protecting the family jewels. They repeatedly told us that when we went to Vietnam, we had to protect our balls. They were forever trying to scare us with stories from Vietnam. One thing that they really wanted us to understand was to cover your balls in combat. They would add by saying, "Do you all want to talk like girls because if you lose your balls, that's what is going to happen." They made predictions about how many of us would be going to Vietnam, and the picture wasn't pretty in terms of statistics.

When I came into the military at the age of nineteen, I was not shaving yet. The army's policy was that if they saw one hair on your face, you were shaving. I had one or two hairs on my face, and because of that, I had to shave quite frequently even though I did not like it. On a daily basis, we also had to dismantle our M14s, clean them, and put them back together again.

I will always remember the first GI party that we had. I thought that we were going to have sodas, ice cream, hot dogs, barbecue, and other treats. Instead, the sergeant drove up to the barracks with wax, mops, brooms, a buffer, and various types of cleaners. This was my introduction to a GI party. One of the most disappointing things about basic training was that when I finished basic training, I was a holdover for thirty days because I did not receive orders to my next duty station (AIT), which stands for Advanced Individual Training. I was to be trained as a combat medic and a surgical technician. Most of the guys moved on to their next duty station, and I never figured out why my assignment didn't come through until thirty days later.

US Army Advanced Individual Training (AIT)

My second duty station was Brooke Army Medical Center, Fort Sam Houston, Texas. Upon arriving at Fort Sam Houston, the base was a little more laid back than what I was used to at Fort Campbell. There was a great deal of activity and many sights to see. To become an army medic and a surgical technician, we had much to learn in the classroom. We marched to every class in formation, and I had a chance to utilize my drumming skills. We marched to class to the beat of a cadence, and I was one of the drummers. After all, I had played the drums in high school. Fort Sam Houston, to me, seemed to have been in the heart of San Antonio, and there was something about the city that was so full of dynamism and intrigue.

Upon arriving at Fort Sam Houston, I was also in for a big culture shock. Brooke Army Medical Center was considered the burn center, and I saw many GIs who had returned from Vietnam with severe burns, missing legs and arms, and some had half of their face blown off. This was a rude awakening for me as well as an introduction to the devastating effects of the Vietnam War.

While at Fort Sam Houston, I felt that my name came up for KP (kitchen police) much too often. It seemed as if I was pulling KP almost every Saturday and Sunday. There were a few soldiers who had church on Saturday because they were Seventh Day Adventists, and they also went home Saturdays for church, at least that's what they professed. I felt used because I felt like they were taking advantage of me, others, and the army.

After being thoroughly trained as a combat medic and a surgical technician, my next duty station was Kimbrough Army Hospital, Fort Meade, Maryland. Our second daughter, Sonia, was born at Kimbrough Army Hospital. While at Kimbrough Army Hospital as a surgical technician, I was exposed to multiple types of surgeries, and I was able to set up the needed equipment used in performing these surgeries.

Many of my friends and acquaintances were receiving orders to go to Vietnam left and right. A good friend who was a medical corpsman received orders to go to Vietnam and paced the floor all night for about two or three weeks. After being deployed in Vietnam for about two weeks, he was killed in combat.

Later, I received orders for Vietnam, and I was supposed to leave around the middle of September and my wife was supposed to deliver our second child. My orders to depart coincided with the delivery date, and I wrote to the Pentagon to try and get an extension. Many people thought that I was crazy for doing this, and they also thought that it would fall on deaf ears. Even though I was trained as a surgical technician (91D20) as well as a combat medic (91A10), my military orders were to go over to Vietnam as a combat medic. This meant that I would be attached to a combat unit and would have to be in actual combat to attend to wounded soldiers. I did receive a letter from the Pentagon, and they told me, "We appreciate your desire to remain with your family at this time and your orders for Vietnam have been put on hold and you will receive amended orders in the near future."

Shortly after, I received orders to go to Germany instead. While in Germany, I worked as a surgical technician at one of the largest military hospitals in Western Europe. After a few months, my family was also able to join me. I arrived in Frankfurt, Germany, in the middle of winter as the snow fell. It reminded me so much of Milwaukee, the place from which I entered the military.

After arriving at the barracks and seeing the hospital in Landstuhl, Germany, I knew that I would like it. The ride on a military bus from Frankfurt to Landstuhl was nothing like the experience I had gone through in basic training. Living in Germany was a tremendous learning experience for me. I did not feel the hurt and the sting of racism that I felt in the United States. In talking to many other black soldiers, they felt the same way. In comparison to the average black person in the United States in the 1970s, the Germans treated you with royalty, deference, and respect. The landscape and terrain were awesome and magnificent, and the roads were winding. The countryside was also breathtaking, and the view was a sight to behold, especially in the fall. In the outlying areas, people lived in villages and the villages were usually about seven to ten miles apart. When my family came over, we lived in the village of Kritchenbach, which reminded you of something from the Middle Ages except that they had cars. Speaking of cars, I owned two Volkswagens while in Germany. One day my car stopped on me and I did not know what the problem was, and almost every adult male in the village of Kritchenbach came out and helped me get my car running, and they did not stop working on it until it started running. I bought a German shepherd dog, and one of the neighbors built a dog house for me. Our dog, whose name was Princess, also was flown back to the United States when I departed.

While working in the operating room, we performed multiple surgeries. We received casualties who were sent to the Second General Hospital before they were sent to the States. Some of the injuries were caused by grenades, AK47s, land mines, and other weapons. We also performed elective surgeries as well as emergency surgeries. I remember one surgery in particular, and this was for a nineteen-year-old black male who was involved in a motorcycle accident. He had multiple broken bones, and they were repaired. As we started to move him from the operating room table to the recovery room cart, he coded (his heart stopped beating) and we tried to resuscitate him but could not. The autopsy revealed that he had a pinhole in his aorta (the largest artery in his body) that was not detected. This artery subsequently ruptured and he died. I'm not sure why, but the image of his face stayed in my mind for years. In fact, the scene is still quite vivid.

Another memorable event in surgery was when a young woman was admitted to the delivery room in her ninth month of pregnancy. I was on call in the operating room along with a nurse and another surgical technician. I was scheduled to be the scrub tech if an emergency case would come upstairs to surgery. This meant that I would have to be gowned and gloved using sterile technique and set up the surgical instruments on the surgical table and pass them to the surgeon as he asked for them. This particular evening (weekend), the obstetrician on call ran up to surgery and informed us to get the operating room ready because he was bringing us a lady who was in labor and was in severe acute distress. He felt that the baby was being suffocated because the umbilical cord was wrapped around the baby's neck like a tightrope. The surgeon looked very panicky and concerned, and he had seconds to minutes to respond.

The patient was wheeled to the operating room by a team of attendants, but we did not have an anesthesiologist to put her asleep because he had not arrived at the hospital yet. He was taking call from home, and he needed time to get to the hospital. The surgical team had no time to wait and an emergency C-section had to be performed on a stat basis. The patient was wheeled through the operating room doors screaming to the top of her voice. She was transferred to the operating room table, and while this was happening, the surgeon was waiting to be gowned and gloved.

A surgical prep to the abdominal area with a surgical soap usually took ten minutes. This time it took all of seven seconds because the surgeon had the surgical nurse spray her abdomen with an iodine spray, and I only had all of two minutes to set up my surgical table with the necessary instruments. There were many instruments needed to perform a C-section, but I had a few seconds to decide what instruments to put on my table and I had a few seconds to do this. The surgeon needed to get this baby out of the mother's uterus as quickly as possible and I knew this. On my table, I placed a scalpel, a suction, scissors, a few sutures, an aspirator to suction the baby's nostrils, sponges, a few hemostats, and an abdominal retractor. The rest of the instruments could wait.

The surgeon asked for a syringe of lidocaine (an anesthetic), and he injected it via a 21-gauge needle directly into the patient's abdomen. As soon as he injected the lidocaine, he asked for the scalpel and started cutting through all of the layers of the abdominal tissue. The anesthetic agent had not completely started to work, but the surgeon had to get this baby out or it would die. The mother was still screaming because she was not fully anesthetized. Thank God, the anesthesiologist arrived and finally put her to sleep. The uterus was opened, and the baby was extricated from the jaws of death, which was having the umbilical cord wrapped around its neck. The baby was already completely blue from a lack of oxygen, but after having the cord released from its neck and suctioning its nostrils, the baby gave out a loud cry and its color turned pink.

At that moment, you could feel the joy and excitement in the room. After surgery, the surgeon thanked the surgical team for its swift action, and he also informed us that the mother and her newborn were doing fine.

While in Germany, I also completed twelve credits through the University of Maryland (European Division). I took two courses in German and two courses in psychology. Living in the village of Kritchenbach, I was also forced to speak German because there was no other American family there. Our two-year-old daughter, Yolanda, was sometimes hard to understand, and the man next door who built the dog house informed me that we could not understand her because she was speaking German. She had a German playmate, and she was automatically picking up German from her. After about a year, I was dreaming in German. There was much to see in Europe, including the concentration camps, and one of my regrets is not traveling more extensively.

It was interesting that even though racism was not detected in the Germans toward blacks, some of the strained differences between black and white Americans continued, even in Germany. The Black Power slogan continued to be heard, and the clenched fist was seen as a common occurrence among black GIs. I heard one of the white enlisted men say to another one, "Every brother (black male) on the hill carries a knife." This was definitely a stereotype because it wasn't true. The Second General Hospital sat on a hill, and this is what the person meant when he mentioned the hill.

After eighteen months of duty, it was time to return to the United States. It was interesting coming through customs in Frankfurt. One of the anesthesiologists had made me a stethoscope to bring back with me. When I went through customs, they took the stethoscope in spite of me telling them that it was a gift. When the plane landed at Fort Dix, New Jersey, I had the saddest feeling in the pit of my stomach, and it was due to having to return to a racist country. The United States of America is the country in which I was born and raised, but I knew that the sting of racism would hit me hard, especially in the South. I thought to myself, *What is wrong with this country—you send us off to fight but yet we return half free?*

After Fort Dix, I was flown to Fort Rucker, Alabama, to be discharged. With two days left in the army, I was reprimanded for not saluting an officer. This incident had me fuming because I thought it was petty. It only reinforced my thoughts and feelings of, *This is America.*

This is a picture of the National Guard Armory in Oak Creek, Wisconsin. In looking out the window from my English class, we could see the guardsmen training. At that time, I was in the eighth grade, and I remember my English teacher saying, "They're not training for nothing, they're going to be deployed to the Republic of Vietnam."

CHAPTER SIX

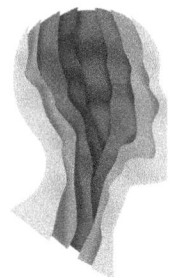

Return to Milwaukee during the "Me Generation"

When I returned back to Milwaukee in the 1970s, I was returning from Alabama after being discharged from the army. It was interesting that even though I entered the army from Wisconsin, I was discharged to Alabama. After my discharge, I stayed in Alabama for two months before driving to Milwaukee, Wisconsin, with my family.

You could still feel the sting of racism in Alabama, even though the schools had been integrated. I knew that I could not live under segregated conditions after being in Germany for almost two years. Family members and other people in the community of Fairhope, Alabama, would say things to me such as, "You can go into that restaurant, they accept black people now," or they would say to me, "Don't go into that restaurant, they're racists and rednecks." It wasn't a good feeling trying to figure out who was a redneck and who wasn't.

Since the schools were integrated now, interracial couples were popping up (mostly black males and white females), but they were for the most part kept on the down low. There were many white males who were civil and polite, but on the other hand, there were many who had a redneck mentality and you didn't know what they would do. Police officers to judges would smile at you, but that didn't mean that they liked you. Hearing a white male's southern accent was an aversion to me, and to this day, I still have an aversion or a negative response to a white male with a southern accent.

Like many black citizens from the South, I made my migration to the North via Interstate 65. Upon arriving in Milwaukee, things were different, but there was still a great deal of racial prejudice. Racial boundaries were still in place, and black people were contained to certain areas of the city. The mayor and the police chief worked in unison to maintain law and order in a city that had already been torn apart and devastated by racial unrest a few years earlier.

In the court system, juvenile and adult black males were receiving unequal treatment by insensitive judges. Their stance was one of punitiveness on every front, and many white citizens expected no less. Racial profiling was blatant, and I truly feel that white police officers in the city of Milwaukee enjoyed stopping black males, and this was especially true on Friday and Saturday nights. Instead of having a good time at a night club on a Friday or a Saturday night, I'm sure many policemen enjoyed giving black males a room for the night, and without saying, that room was a jail cell. Being a black male, I always felt like the police department had a sting operation going, and this was directed at every black male. Many of the black males who lived in Milwaukee may have been born in the South, and instead of running to freedom, many hit a brick wall. The inner cities and ghettos look the same in every major city in the United States, and it is no accident that this happened.

After arriving in Milwaukee, Mr. Ervin Pitts and Mrs. Arletha Pitts, his wife, allowed me and my family to live with them for six months. I had brought from Germany a German shepherd dog (Princess), whom they accepted into their home as well. Ervin and Arletha also grew up in my hometown, Fairhope, Alabama, and they, too, felt the sting of racism in Alabama and Milwaukee. I am very appreciative to them for being a big brother and a big sister to me.

When I was applying for a job as a surgical technician, I put in several applications at local hospitals, and the phone was ringing for offers before I even returned home. I chose to work at St. Joseph's

Hospital, and I started out working days but soon went to third shift. Also, in six months, I had purchased my first home that both my wife and I were proud of. I have fond memories of this home, even though this is where the dissolution of my marriage took place.

I truly enjoyed working as a surgical technician, and I was proud of my skills. I had been trained by the army, and I feel that my skills were exceptional. I also felt that I had seen every surgical procedure that there was to see. The surgeons felt comfortable with my skills, and I was always complimented by surgeons from many specialty areas.

One morning, I was assigned to be the scrub tech on a craniotomy. I think the patient had a tumor on the brain, and the surgeon was operating to remove the tumor. I had no problem setting up the case and preparing the various instruments that would be needed because I had seen so many of these procedures while in the army. We also had to do many craniotomies on an emergency basis while in the army, and there were times when I had only ten or fifteen minutes to set up before the surgeon was asking for the saw to cut through the skull. I knew the names of all of the instruments on the table, and I knew what they were used for.

On this particular morning at St. Joseph's Hospital, the neurosurgeon walked in the room and saw me and went ballistic. He didn't know me, but one thing was for sure, he made it clear that he did not want me to be the scrub tech on his case. He yelled and screamed and threw a tantrum and called in the operating room supervisor. While this commotion was going on, the anesthesiologist stood straight up, pointed his finger at the surgeon, and said, "You have no reason to treat him like that, he is an excellent technician, and you're out of line." The anesthesiologist was angry, and he did not have to defend me but he did. It is important for all of us to take a stand when we see another person being wronged. In a lifetime, some things we forget but the surgeon's reaction to me and the anesthesiologist's support, I will never forget. I think that at that time people were not used to black faces in skilled positions. Also, there were about two other black faces in the operating room.

As a third shift surgical technician, I would come to work at 11:00 p.m. and get off at 7:00 a.m. An RN worked along with me, and we would have to cover the operating room and the emergency room. I chose to work the third shift because I attended school full-time during the day.

Many days I went straight to class and I wasn't done with classes until around 3:00 p.m. It was also hard to go right to sleep when I got home because I was so wound up. Most of the time, I would fall asleep around 6:00 or 7:00 p.m., and it was time to get up again at 10:00 p.m. to go back to work. I kept this schedule for about two years, and this is something that I would never do again. Whenever my clients tell me that they work this shift and they have kids, my body starts to tremble. My original intent was to become an obstetrician-gynecologist, but when I took general psychology in college, my focus shifted. I became curious about human nature and psychology seemed like it was right for me, but this would also be put on hold.

When I was working the third shift, one night I had to set up for an emergency appendectomy. While the emergency appendectomy was in progress on the third floor, I received news that my wife had been brought in at about 3:30 a.m., and she was in the delivery room on the second floor just beneath us. She gave birth to a nine-pound boy, Earl Jr., at about 4:00 a.m. It was a normal delivery, and as I stood there assisting with the appendectomy, I wasn't worried because I knew that she was in good hands.

Dr. William Finlayson, a black doctor, was her doctor, and I had done many C-sections with him. As the first black doctor there, I didn't always think that he was treated fairly by some of the other white doctors. He always carried himself with a great deal of pride and dignity, and he had a strong resemblance to Dr. Martin Luther King.

While I was working the third shift one night, I was assisting on a C-section. The patient was black, and the surgeon cut the umbilical cord and handed the newborn to the pediatrician. His comment was, "This is another one for the welfare." The whole room broke out in laughter, and this was just one of many times that I felt invisible and humiliated. What surprised me most was that I did not expect these words to come from this particular surgeon.

On another occasion, while working in the emergency room on the third shift, the nurse called the attending doctor to let him know that a female patient was waiting to see him. The patient was experiencing abdominal pain, and the first question that the attending physician asked was, "Is she black?" In finding out that she was black, his response was "Oh, shit!" He said this because he did not want to deal with a Title 19 patient (welfare). This same physician went in to talk to another patient on a different occasion, and the patient was black and on Title 19. After ordering a shot of penicillin for her, which may have been for an STD, he also gave her some pills, but he did not fully explain to her why he was giving her pills.

The question that the patient asked was, "What should I do with these?" As he closed the door to her room, he responded, "Take them and stick them up your ass, bitch." Historically, many black people have not trusted doctors, and they have not known that it is important to have a family doctor, and through no fault of their own, they never fully understood proper use of the emergency room. Emergency room doctors should also be more understanding and compassionate in treating black patients or any patient.

On a different occasion, a different doctor who was covering the emergency room on the third shift was seeing a white female patient for abdominal pain, and he jokingly came over and whispered in my ear and said, "If she was black, I would call it pelvic inflammatory disease, but since she is white, I'm going to call it a urinary tract infection." He then laughed and walked away. The Hippocratic Oath tells doctors to "First, let us do no harm," and we have to make sure that this oath is adhered to.

Working in the medical field, I learned that if you're black, you're thought to be on Title 19 until you prove otherwise. As a black medical professional, working in the operating room, I had the opportunity to observe things firsthand. The following are a list of statements made in my presence:

1. At 7:00 a.m., I asked a white physician how was his night after he worked the third shift in the ER, and he stated, "I was up all night taking care of your people."
2. The same physician on another occasion stated, "These black welfare women, they are so stupid."

3. A question was asked of me by a white male patient. He wanted to know, "How did a black man become interested in medicine?" About ten years later, while doing my internship in psychology, a white male intern asked me again, "How did you become interested in psychology?" It's unfortunate that black males have to go through such humiliation.
4. An anesthesiologist stated to me, "If everyone was like you, I wouldn't have anything to worry about." What he was saying was, "I don't trust black people."
5. After flying to San Diego, California, with a group of physicians, we got off of a shuttle bus that was to take us to the hotel. Everyone who got on the shuttle bus was white except me. After everyone was seated, the driver turned around and in a sharp and abrasive voice asked me, "Hey, where's your ticket?" Again, an anesthesiologist, Dr. William Mateicka, came to my rescue. Before I could say anything, Dr. Mateicka said to him in a stern and authoritative voice, "He's with us!"
6. One day at St. Luke's Hospital, I spoke to a surgical resident (doctor) around the noon hour. I asked him how he was doing, and he stated with a straight face, "We were out to lunch talking about niggers." My regret is that I did not report him to the chief of the department of surgery.
7. While working in the emergency room one night, a police officer was asked by a nurse if he could transport a client and his comment was, "If we can do it for inner city (black) residents, we can do it for anybody." You could also tell that they had a great disdain for inner city residents.
8. A surgeon said to a surgical resident as he was sewing up the patient's skin, "Don't worry about doing anything fancy since she's not paying for it anyway." The patient was on Title 19.

As an educated black male living in Milwaukee and having worked in the medical field, I would have some reservations about walking into any emergency room in the city. The thought that would come to my mind would be, *How do the physician and the emergency room staff perceive me?* I would also be asking myself these questions:

1. Do they think that I'm malingering?
2. Do they wonder why I waited so long?
3. Do they wonder if I have a job?
4. Do they wonder if I have insurance?
5. Will the staff be rude and condescending?
6. Will they assume that I am uneducated?
7. If the physician is foreign-born, will he or she afford me the dignity and respect that I deserve?

I left St. Joseph's Hospital and took a position at St. Luke's Hospital. Before leaving St. Joseph's Hospital, I decided to give the army a try again by joining the Army Reserve. I joined a medical unit, and we trained one weekend per month. Within a short time, I was disillusioned about this unit because prejudice and discrimination were rampant. During the one weekend a month when we met, some or most of the white guys would sequester themselves in their quarters and watch television, play cards, and read *Playboy* magazines. If the black reservists tried to join them, the doors were locked so that the black guys could not gain entrance.

During our two weeks of reserve training, we went to Camp McCoy in Tomah, Wisconsin, and that again was a bad experience. After being on the base for less than an hour, I was walking with another black reservist, and two white MPs passed us and yelled out something to the effect that we were walking on the wrong side of the road. Since we didn't move fast enough, they made a U-turn in their OD army green Jeep. One was hostile and abrasive, and the other one seemed nice and didn't say anything. The hostile one appeared to be looking for a confrontation, and he told us that we were violating post policy by not walking on the right side of the highway. My friend did not say anything, but I became enraged because I "smelled a rat." My gut told me that this was harassment because we were black, and the hostile MP knew that we had just gotten on base.

He went on to say that it was a violation to walk on the wrong side of the road, and I found myself getting angrier by the minute. My next response was, "It's not a road, it's a street." This must have upset him because he then told me to turn around, spread my legs, and stretch my arms out on the Jeep. I was feeling more humiliated and dehumanized as the seconds ticked. I thought to myself, *I was in the army on active duty for three years and never got into any trouble, and I join the reserves and I find myself in this predicament.* I felt my whole body become tense and rigid as he struggled to handcuff me. I felt that I had not done anything to be handcuffed, and the adrenaline was starting to kick in.

As I think back on this unfortunate incident, I could not help but think about black males that were shot because they were "resisting arrest." I remember being handcuffed, thrown in the back of the Jeep, and taken to the stockade. I remember going before the company commander and explaining my story to him, and it seemed like he wasn't sure who he wanted to believe. I left there thinking that he wanted to side with the MP, but my story was credible and he had to examine his conscience and do the right thing. I went on to tell the company commander that I had just gotten on base, and I had no idea of what side of the street I should have been walking on. I also informed the company commander that I had received an honorable discharge from the regular army and that I had never gotten into any trouble while on active duty. In fact, I had helped make a training film that was part of the army's archives. They were able to retrieve this training film, and the company commander and other officers viewed it and were impressed. At this point, they started treating me in a much more positive light. They then put me on duty as a medic in the emergency room, and one night we received a call to respond to a car accident whereby someone had flipped their car over. We left the emergency room with our lights and sirens blasting. When we arrived on the scene, little did I know that the same MP on the scene of the accident who was directing traffic and securing the area was the same MP who had arrested me earlier. As Martin Luther King said, "We are all tied together in a mutual destiny." As human beings, inhabiting this earth, we need to always respect one another.

Also, we never really know how our lives will cross. Before leaving the stockade, I remember the company commander having the both of us shake hands, and during the two weeks at Camp McCoy, I remember running into the same MP and we waved at each other in a cordial manner each time our paths crossed.

On another occasion, we attended a bivouac where we slept outside in tents. This occurred in West Bend, Wisconsin. The first thing that I sensed was a great deal of racial polarization again. While on bivouac on a Saturday night, I remember the carloads of white reservists going into the downtown area of West Bend. They were actually going to drink at a club, and they made sure that no black guys tagged along. In retrospect, I don't think that I would have wanted to go and walk into the uncomfortable environment of a redneck bar. At that time, West Bend, Wisconsin, was not ready to accept black people, and I think the white reservists knew it.

After arriving back in Milwaukee, I spoke to a white staff sergeant and I told him I no longer wanted to be a reservist and I informed him that it was because of all of the racism I felt. He called me a few weeks later and told me that things had changed and asked if I would reconsider. I had reached a saturation point, and I just needed to get out.

I failed to mention that I received an associate degree in liberal arts from Milwaukee Area Technical College while working third shift full-time and attending school full-time and maintaining a family.

In addition to jobs in the medical profession, I also delivered papers for the *Wall Street Journal*, the *Chicago Tribune*, and the *Milwaukee Journal*, and I also worked as a paramedic with Bell Ambulance.

The 1970s were an interesting decade. It was a decade of the women's liberation movement, and women were initiating divorces in a way that had never happened before. This shift was also found in my own life. Job wise, I switched from St. Joseph's Hospital to St. Luke's Hospital. I worked four years as a surgical technician at St. Luke's before being trained as a cardiovascular perfusionist. Being a perfusionist puts a tremendous strain on a marriage, and this will be discussed in a later section.

My marriage lasted twelve years, and out of those twelve years, about two and a half years were happy years. Communication is important in any relationship, and I feel that a lack of communication destroyed my marriage. In the 1970s and 1980s, there was a tendency for many couples to go out by themselves, and women were more inclined to go out with their friends. This shift was confusing for men, and there was this type of competitiveness that set in between men and women. I was always envious but happy for couples who were able to hold their marriage together.

There was sort of a "tit for tat" going on between couples. It was common for the woman to say for example, "You went out with your friends two times last week, so now don't question me when I go out with my friends." I guess you could say that we were truly the young and the restless. I can also truly say that my psychology career started late because emotionally I had to find out who I really was. Sometimes we put roadblocks in our path because we don't allow ourselves to let go of excess baggage that holds us back. It is also important to know who you are and to accept who you are.

There are so many black men who tend to wear a mask, and they hide behind the mask of pain, hurt, anger, disappointment, rejection, and marginalization. As men, we need to be in touch with our inner feelings and know who we are. Sometimes it takes other people to help us see the light and to help us recognize our full potential. I enrolled myself in therapy with a very good therapist, who helped me through my divorce, and he helped me to realize that I could be a psychologist myself. Black people still harbor stigmas about therapy, and this is something that they should let go of. I truly believe that Michael Jackson would have been much better off with a psychologist rather than a cardiologist.

In the early years of my marriage, the emotional turmoil that was experienced caused problems in my ability to concentrate. Family interference was also another issue and having family members and especially in-laws moving in can destroy a marriage. There is a tendency for family members to also engage in a lot of "he said, she said" talk, and this definitely strains an already fragile marriage.

When my divorce took place, I was angry at my wife's attorney, and letting go of my marriage was extremely difficult. I remember crying like a baby, but my crying was in vain. My wife, Olivia, was not budging, and she was not changing her mind. I think people go through a grieving process and divorce can be similar to death, but in my case my ex-wife was walking around and I could see her and that was the most hurting part.

One way to comprehend this would be to think of a child who is separated from his mother, and whenever the child sees the mother, the child's behavior declines and the child starts to act out. Whenever I saw my ex-wife, I acted like this child. My pride was shattered and people would always come up to me and ask me, "How did you let that fine woman get away from you?"

People have many reasons for getting divorced, and negative statements should not be made toward either party. It took me some time to get over my divorce, but once I got over it, I was at peace. Stupid people would always make stupid comments such as, "The problem must have been in the bedroom." You have to be big enough to rise above the derisive comments; otherwise, you get pulled into a negative mind-set that does more damage than good. Above all else, you want to be able to keep the "self" intact.

I think that in the 1970s women wanted to be liberated, and I have a hunch that many men experienced what I experienced.

My ex-wife and I have always communicated, and this is important for the well-being of the children. I can truly say that it was therapy that put me on the right path to communicate with my ex-wife. This, however, did not happen overnight. It took a couple of years, but since that time, my communication with her has been constant and positive. Many people think that because we get along so well that I am still in love with her. The truth of the matter is I respect her, and she is the mother of my children, and I will always elevate her because to do otherwise hurts the children and it makes me look like a real jerk. Children struggle as it is with a divorce, and oftentimes the pain follows them into adulthood. Also, life is forever changing, and change can be hard for adults and children. Today, I implore parents to communicate in a positive manner for their own well-being and for the emotional stability of their children.

In the 1980s, I started working as a cardiovascular perfusionist at St. Luke's Hospital. I was trained to become a perfusionist, and this job was quite demanding. Another name for a cardiovascular perfusionist is someone who operates the heart-lung machine while patients undergo open-heart surgery. During my career, I operated the heart-lung machine on approximately three thousand open-heart cases.

When I started working as a perfusionist, I worked with about six open-heart surgeons. World-renowned surgeon Dr. Dudley Johnson was the head heart surgeon, and this job was quite demanding. When you operate the heart-lung machine, you have to be fully alert at all times. This job is similar to that of an airline pilot. Pilots have a checklist that they have to go through before they take off and land. When flying a plane, the first eleven minutes after takeoff and the last eleven minutes prior to landing are the most critical. Likewise, when operating the heart-lung machine, the period when you're putting the patient on the heart-lung machine and when you're bringing the patient off the heart-lung machine are the most critical. There should be very few distractions, and each movement made by the perfusionist should be precise, methodical, and meticulous.

When operating the heart-lung machine, the patient's heart is stopped and the blood is diverted from the heart to the heart-lung machine, and the heart-lung machine is functioning as the heart and lungs. It is also called extracorporeal circulation because the blood is rerouted outside of the body. Before the patient goes on the heart-lung machine, heparin is given to the patient by the anesthesiologist, and a loading dose is put into the heart-lung machine. Usually, a loading dose is ten to fifteen thousand units depending on a patient's weight. Heparin is a drug that prevents the blood from clotting or coagulating. If heparin is not given prior to cardiopulmonary bypass or heart surgery, the heart-lung machine could clot off, and this could be instant death for the patient. Fortunately, this is something that never happened to me during my long career as a cardiovascular perfusionist. Whenever it was time to bring the patient off of the heart-lung machine, the anesthesiologist would give a dose of protamine sulfate, and this would cause the patient's blood to come back to its original state. Many people use the terms coagulation or clotting, so it's important to measure fibrinogen levels and prothrombin times to assess whether or not the patient will have a bleeding problem after surgery. If the levels are where they should be, the patient can be closed and moved on to the intensive care unit.

As a perfusionist, I was never called into court, for any type of litigation, and I never had to sit through a deposition. As a psychologist, I am in court all the time due to the nature of my work. People ask me all the time, "What's more stressful, perfusion or psychology?" It is definitely psychology, and I will explain why, later in the book.

When putting the patient on the heart-lung machine, the surgeon can stop the patient's heart from beating by putting an electrode on the heart that is called a fibrillator, and this can stop the heart from beating or put it in a state of asystole. After the heart is arrested, a cardioplegic (paralyzing agent) solution is injected into the root of the aorta that travels through the coronary arteries. Usually the cardioplegic solution included potassium, magnesium sulfate, glucose, a bicarbonate, or other solutions. These solutions caused immediate arrest of the heart, hypothermia, membrane stabilization, and prevented edema or swelling. The heart-lung machine also had the capacity to cool the patient's body temperature down to whatever temperature the surgeon wanted it to be. Generally, the patient's temperature was dropped to ninety degrees Fahrenheit or lower, and when the procedure was completed, the patient was rewarmed to ninety-eight degrees. While on the heart-lung machine, the perfusionist maintained the patient's blood gases and made sure that they were within normal limits. We kept the patient oxygenated by maintaining an oxygen saturation of 98 to 100 percent and a venous saturation of around 80. We also had to keep track of clotting times, bicarbonate levels, oxygen levels, carbon dioxide levels, pH levels, the hematocrit or hemoglobin levels, and providing a constant vapor anesthetic to keep the patient asleep.

There were many days that I worked eighteen to twenty hours per day. There were also times when I would get home at 3:00 a.m. in the morning and would have to return to the operating room at

5:00 a.m. to set the heart-lung machine up for a 7:00 a.m. case. We were expected to wait for the surgeon, but the surgeon did not like waiting for the perfusionist. Whenever I was able to get four hours of sleep, I felt that that was a bonus.

During the 1980s, which was the heyday of heart surgery, surgeons worked around the clock, and some of them were also having heart attacks. Heart surgeons also remind me a lot of judges. Judges like to be in control of their courtroom, and heart surgeons like to be in control of the operating room. Like judges, they can also turn serious very quickly. Heart surgeons will sometimes present with two personalities. You can converse with them in the doctor's lounge and they can be very cordial and civil, but when they gown and glove and stand over the patient's chest, all hell can break loose. They can be demeaning, condescending, and abrasive to everyone in the operating room. After working with surgeons for such a long time, I understood that they were the captain of the ship and they have a patient's life on the table that they're responsible for. If something goes wrong in surgery, the surgeon is the one who has to talk to the family, and at all times he is under a tremendous amount of pressure. If he or she runs into an unexpected anomaly or profuse bleeding that is extremely difficult to control, the surgeon may scream and yell and curse you out, but after everything is under control, he'll ask you to turn on some classical or country music and he'll start cracking jokes or say complimentary things to the nurses or technicians.

After working as a perfusionist for Dr. Dudley Johnson, I was asked by Dr. Richard T. Shore, another gifted heart surgeon, to work for him when he split off from Dr. Johnson. This split took place in the early 1980s, and I became a perfusionist for Dr. Richard T. Shore. We worked at several hospitals such as St. Luke's of Milwaukee, Wisconsin, St. Mary's, Sinai Samaritan, Columbia, and Mount Sinai. Dr. Shore was extremely dedicated to his patients, and he was good to his employees. As a black man, he trusted me to operate the heart-lung machine on his patients, and it is important to note that many of his patients came from across the country to have Dr. Shore operate on them because of his results and his reputation. Dr. Shore was my mentor, and he took me under his wing and provided expert tutelage. There were times when he was ostracized and there were times when others questioned my qualifications, but he stood firmly behind me. It was very interesting to be in an operating room, being the only black most of the time and having such a key role in the procedure. Sometimes people would look in awe, and I'm sure they wondered why Dr. Shore picked me. Just like a psychologist has to take a national board exam, perfusionists also had to take a national board exam that consisted of about two hundred difficult multiple choice questions. Before I passed my perfusion boards, many people would ask me if I was certified. They knew that I had not passed my boards yet, and they were asking because they wanted to rub it in and humiliate me. When I passed my boards, people then stopped asking me. While working for Dr. Shore, I also finished my BA in psychology and went on to graduate school. When I told him that I wanted to attend graduate school, I think he was taken aback but he acquiesced.

Some of my coworkers did not like the idea of me going to school because it meant more work for them, but Dr. Shore made it clear to the team that I would be returning to school and he expected 100 percent cooperation. When I started graduate school, I resigned from the group for six months and I had plenty of time to study. I drove from Milwaukee to the Chicago area three days per week, and I missed what I had been doing but I loved school, and when I was into the books, I felt like a kid in a candy store. I feel that we are meant to be at certain places in life, and people do come into our lives for a reason. Dr. Shore was truly one in a million, and to me he was an employer, a mentor, and a friend.

When I started graduate school, I worked part-time in perfusion for a while but slowly phased out of it. The first day of class gave me a great deal of anticipatory anxiety, and as I drove to the Chicago area from Milwaukee, I felt fragmented, as if half of me was in Milwaukee and the other half was in Illinois. I was changing and I had to let go of the old Earl, and I'm not sure if I was quite ready to do that but I had to. This is something that actually reminded me of something that happened in the operating room, having to do with being ready to take charge. One day I was first assisting Dr. Shore as he prepared to put a cannula into the patient's aorta, which was one procedure necessary to hook the patient up to the heart-lung machine. I had done this many times before, but I had not done it recently because there was always a physician's assistant around. This particular day we did not have one, so I was called from the heart-lung machine to the table to assist Dr. Shore. As he was cannulating, his hands were moving quite fast, and he was getting perturbed because I could not keep up. I said to him, "I'm not used to being in this position," and his comment was, "Well, you're here now." What he was telling me was that he was expecting me to perform. Likewise, when I was driving to Illinois the first day of graduate school, I could have said to myself, "Well, you're here now."

Before graduate school, I attended very few funerals, but during graduate school I attended eighteen funerals. During my first year of graduate school, my uncle, my father's brother Claude, died.

He was a kind man, and I remember all of the kind things that he did for me when I was a kid and an adult. The second person to die was my sister, Joyce Lewis, who was the oldest. She died from breast cancer, and her faith in God was very strong. Toward the end of her life, she said to me, "Baby brother, don't waste your money on phone calls calling me. If anything happens, I'll let you know." My sister went into a coma and was taken to the hospital at about 2:00 a.m. one morning. She did let me know because at about 2:00 a.m. the same morning, I jumped straight up out of bed and my heart was pounding, but I did not know why. She did say that she would let me know if anything happened. She died later that day, but she still had control. The family in Alabama had gathered in her room, and they were waiting for her daughter, Vickie, to get to the hospital from Atlanta. Vickie actually had to race to make it to the hospital. When Vickie did get to the hospital, someone in the family announced that Vickie was getting off the elevator. My sister heard them say this, and she took her last breath.

When we had her funeral, it was held at the church that we all attended as children. This church sits right in front of our house. On the day of the funeral, family and friends gathered at our house, and there were so many people until it was hard to move. I remember that it was a hot day in July, and the sky was completely blue without a cloud. As I stood among a crowd of people, in the family room, I looked up at the sky and saw a perfect formation of white birds flying in a V shape right over the church. The hearse had just pulled up to take her casket into the church, and it was as if she was getting a special salute. I know what I saw and I know that I was not hallucinating. When I was able to get past the people and get outside to get a better view of the birds, I did not see them. I will always believe that my sister was telling me that she was OK.

My mother was still in shock and she said upon seeing the casket being removed from the hearse, "She can't breathe." She was referring to my sister. During the viewing, my mother started speaking in tongues, and I noticed that when my father went to view her body, he made it halfway and his knees seemed to have buckled. He had always said to me, "We didn't come to this earth to stay," and I was actually expecting a different reaction from him. My mother also lost two brothers while I was in graduate school, and I was able to attend one funeral. One of my other sisters lost a son who had some anomalies from birth, and a close friend of mine lost her father and two uncles, and I attended all of these funerals plus three others who were unrelated to me.

My uncle Wilmer Matherson, whom I lived with in Oak Creek, Wisconsin, died midway through graduate school. He became ill and was in and out of Mount Sinai Hospital in Milwaukee. Mount Sinai was also called Sinai Aurora, which is located in the downtown area and the heart of the inner city. Aurora St. Luke's is on the south side of Milwaukee, and there is a pronounced distinction between the two hospitals. Most doctors, I can assure you, would prefer to operate at Aurora St. Luke's. In the past, many black patients came to Mount Sinai, and I truly believe that the treatment was substandard. When I was working as a perfusionist, I was in the heart catheterization lab waiting for a patient to be cathed, and a physician on the case casually made a comment about black people. His comment was pertaining to the rate of heart disease, strokes, diabetes, and kidney disease that's found in African Americans. He stated, "It's all those guts and all that other junk that they eat." He was probably referring to everything on the pig and some.

While my uncle was at Mount Sinai, he had a rocky recovery after the heart surgery. The people who worked there seemed cold, presumptuous, and distant. There was one nurse in particular who stood out from the rest. She was a white nurse who was caring, compassionate, and humane. I went so far as to send her a card to let her know how much I appreciated her dedication and the excellent way in which she took care of my uncle.

Graduate school can be grueling, and because of that, I did not get to the hospital to see my uncle as much as I wanted to. Also, I was driving back and forth from Milwaukee to Chicago to school. My uncle's son, Kevin, also spent a great deal of time with my uncle. After having his heart surgery, my uncle suffered a stroke but recuperated nicely. One night, while in his hospital room, he suffered a cardiac arrest and was resuscitated. His vital signs started to weaken, and according to the doctors, his brain was not functioning. A team of about ten or twelve physicians summoned the family and told us that if we wanted to see him, do it now because he would slowly diminish and death was imminent. I left the hospital that night, got a good night's sleep, and went back early the next morning. Before I left the house, I couldn't think of anything else to do, so I prayed and I opened the bible, not looking for any particular scripture. I started reading the first page that came up, and it was John, chapter 11, where Jesus said, "Lazarus, come out." He came out, his hands and feet wrapped in grave cloths and with a cloth around his face. "Untie him," Jesus told them, "and let him go." I could have opened the Bible to any chapter, but this is the chapter that came up.

When I walked into my uncle's room of the intensive care unit, I was expecting to see a lifeless body. Instead, his skin had excellent color, and when I looked at the urimeter, he was putting out a steady flow of clear urine, and as a perfusionist I knew these were good signs. I looked at his EKG, and his blood pressure was normal and his EKG was in perfect rhythm. He started to open his eyes, and he certainly did not look like a man who was dying. Blood gases were taken, and they were all within the normal range. The doctors were baffled, and they didn't have an explanation for what happened, but my uncle recuperated, went home, and lived for another six months.

He was quite coherent, and he was able to communicate effectively with very little difficulty.

I was preparing for my comprehensive exams, which are taken midway through graduate school, and on the day that I sat down to take this exam was the day that my uncle died. I started to feel that every time I made a gain, there was a setback.

My other uncle, Mr. Claude Matherson, was the brother of my uncle who had just died. Uncle Claude died in 1990, and about two weeks before Uncle Wilmer died, my uncle Claude came to me in a dream. In the dream, he had a big smile on his face, but he did not utter a word. I am also into dream interpretation, and my interpretation of the dream was that he was simply saying, "You've done the best that you can do, let him go."

My uncle was a Rudyard Kipling to me. When I was a boy and when I became a man, he talked to me like Rudyard Kipling spoke in the poem "If," which follows:

> IF you can keep your head when all about you
> Are losing theirs and blaming it on you,
> If you can trust yourself when all men doubt you,
> But make allowance for their doubting too;
> If you can wait and not be tired by waiting,
> Or being lied about, don't deal in lies,
> Or being hated, don't give way to hating,
> And yet don't look too good, nor talk too wise:
>
> If you can dream—and not make dreams your master;
> If you can think—and not make thoughts your aim;
> If you can meet with Triumph and Disaster
> And treat those two impostors just the same;
> If you can bear to hear the truth you've spoken
> Twisted by knaves to make a trap for fools,
> Or watch the things you gave your life to, broken,
> And stoop and build 'em up with worn-out tools:
> If you can make one heap of all your winnings
> And risk it on one turn of pitch-and-toss,

And lose, and start again at your beginnings
And never breathe a word about your loss;
If you can force your heart and nerve and sinew
To serve your turn long after they are gone,
And so hold on when there is nothing in you
Except the Will which says to them: "Hold on!"
If you can talk with crowds and keep your virtue,
Or walk with Kings—nor lose the common touch,
if neither foes nor loving friends can hurt you,
If all men count with you, but none too much;
If you can fill the unforgiving minute
With sixty seconds' worth of distance run,
Yours is the Earth and everything that's in it,
And—which is more—you'll be a Man, my son!

Another death that affected me deeply was the death of my mentor, Dr. Richard T. Shore, a gifted heart surgeon that I worked for, for many years as before mentioned. He gave me expert tutelage and advice, and he also came into my life for a reason.

As a psychologist, I believe that dreams can tell us many things if we listen to them. One night I had a very powerful dream about Dr. Shore. In the dream, I saw him coming out of a large body of water, and he was walking toward the shore. He had on just a pair of trunks, and it appeared also that he had cuts on his legs, and he was holding his chest with one hand. His face was filled with confusion, pain, hurt, dismay, and agony. Shortly after the dream, Dr. Shore's twenty-nine-year-old son drowned in the Potomac River, and his body surfaced approximately two weeks later with some lacerations to the body. Approximately a year later, in 1995 on Christmas Eve, Dr. Shore died at his home of a massive heart attack. I believe that what took place in my dream was a premonition. In my dream, when he surfaced from the water with cuts, this somehow represented his son's death, and the fact that he was holding his chest foretold his heart attack. Having this ability to dream certain things is not pleasant for me, but it has been a part of me for as long as I can remember.

The deaths of Dr. Shore and his son were tragic and hurtful to all who knew them. This gifted surgeon who left us too soon saved thousands of patients, and when other surgeons readily gave up on resuscitating a patient, Dr Shore never gave up. If a patient was past critical, he still gave it his all, and he tried every technique that he could think of to save a patient. Ironically, there was no one there to save him. Because of his death on Christmas Eve, 1995, my episodic memory will not allow me to fully enjoy Christmas, even to this day.

Dr. Shore was a surgeon who never gave up on his patients. He operated on the sickest of the sick. and he exhibited a great deal of compassion and perseverance, and he expected no less from the entire surgical team. In addition to teaching medical personnel the technical skills that are needed, they should also be taught empathy and the importance of perseverance and determination when a patient's life hangs in the balance. Most surgeons and anesthesiologists worked diligently to save their patients, but I saw other ancillary personnel who would have rather seen the surgeon pronounce a patient dead than see this surgeon work tirelessly in trying to revive a patient. Some medical personnel would have been more content, sitting in the nonphysicians' lounge all night or going home early rather than working overtime to save a patient's life.

Sometimes egos would clash as well. While working in the emergency room one night, a person was brought in DOA (dead on arrival), and a priest was in the room administering the last rites. A Jewish doctor who was attending the emergency room was waiting outside the decedent's room to pronounce him, but while waiting, the Jewish doctor became very angry and irate because he had to wait on the priest to finish.

As a black male working in the surgical arena, it was unfortunate but you always felt as if an insult was coming your way at any moment. One of my fellow workers made a comment to a doctor in training from Eastern Europe that the only people in the world who had not made a contribution to society were black people. This was indeed an ignorant statement, and it may be a mind-set that hundreds of thousands of other people have as well. One other male at a different hospital had been trained as a surgical technician in the navy, and on this particular evening, his wife had brought their three-year-old daughter into the nurse's lounge. When I walked in, the technician said to his daughter, "Don't worry, honey, he's one of the good ones." It appears that he may have been teaching his daughter that many black people are bad. In fact, one day an anesthesiologist asked me, "How come everybody is not like you?"

In meeting an intelligent black person, many white people may still feel that this is an aberration rather than the norm. When Jeffrey Dahmer murdered his victims, a technician stated, "There's no loss because they were not going to go to college anyway. "

After finding out that I wanted to go to medical school, another physician told me that I should have lots of kids. I wasn't exactly sure what he meant, but I had the distinct feeling that he was concerned about enhancing the gene pool. In other words, he may have been saying, "You seem like an intelligent guy, therefore, your children will be intelligent." On the other hand, another physician was talking to me about medical school, and he went on to say, "We can't find any blacks who are qualified to get into medical school." At that point he let out a loud roar of "Ha! Ha! Ha!" I don't know the exact number of black doctors in the United States, but medical schools are graduating hundreds if not thousands per year.

In the 1970s and the 1980s, it's interesting that the mind-set of most of white America was so skewed and flawed. While in the operating room, people tend to hold very interesting conversations. When Harold Washington was elected mayor of Chicago, a physician commented, "Chicago has now gone to the dogs." My personal assessment is that Mayor Washington did a superb job in managing the city of Chicago. In fact, he sacrificed his life for a city that he loved. On another occasion, a surgical resident who was also a former nun commented to the chief of surgery when talking about Gary, Indiana. Her comment was, "It snows brown in Gary." Because she had been a nun, her comment totally shocked me. In making this statement, she was referring to the filth and blight that she felt defined Gary, Indiana.

A person should not have to live with repetitive personal attacks or attacks against black people in general, but I grew to expect these attacks and I never knew when or who they were coming from. A group of people from the operating room went out to a bar one night, and a male nurse said to one of the male medical technicians, "You need to put on some more clothes. You're dressed just like a nigger," and it did not faze the nurse that I was standing there. I then started asking myself more and more, "How can you live in a country and not feel like you're part of it?"

It seemed like everywhere I turned, there was this sting of racism. The operating room personnel had a picnic in Cudahy Park in Cudahy, Wisconsin, and we were all sitting around having a good time eating barbecue and drinking beer for which we had a permit. There were at least thirty or forty people there, and out of nowhere two white males drove up on motorcycles. They both looked mean and angry, and they identified themselves as police officers even though they were not in uniform. They walked past all of the other people and came straight to me and wanted to know where my permit was. I was the only black person in the group, and right away, a nurse came to my rescue and stated, "I have the permit." She seemed very nervous and shaken by the chain of events, and at that moment, I felt that many of the people there felt the impact of injustice and racism. The two men on the motorcycles drove off, but they both glared at me with disdain before leaving.

Lastly, one day in the mid-1970s, I decided that I wanted to find a dentist outside of the Milwaukee area. I located a dentist in Brookfield, Wisconsin, which is considered to be an exclusive suburb of Milwaukee. The first question the dentist asked me was, "Why didn't you go to a dentist in your area?" After a while, as a black person you don't know what you feel anymore. One thing is for sure, you feel a tremendous amount of anger and doubt as a person. The important thing is to take this anger and use it to elevate yourself whereby you're able not only to help yourself but others as well. Before I became a psychologist, I took many mental notes regarding my personal experiences and the things that were said to me or around me.

Previously, I stated that I have an aversion to white males with a southern accent, but I have to say that I went to a white male dentist at the VA Hospital who had a southern accent, and he imparted some words to me that I never forgot. In talking about all of the racial hatred and bigotry, he stated, "Sometimes I think God put us on earth just to see how big of a fool we could make out of ourselves."

In regards to dealing with rage and anger, it is appalling the number of black males who simply become defeated and give up. They may oftentimes put themselves in the position to be killed or they may self-destruct by abusing drugs or alcohol.

I overheard a conversation of black men talking in a restaurant, and I discovered that they have a genuine fear of being stopped by or abused by the police. This feeling of not being safe stems back to their childhood growing up in the Deep South. Another retired black gentleman stated that he feels very uncomfortable in restaurants whenever he goes home to Arkansas. These feelings emanate from a childhood schema whereby the person knew that they were breaking the law if they went into a white establishment, and this schema or belief has followed them into adulthood. For this reason, this gentleman stated that he carries a gun with him whenever he's in Arkansas. This is a prime example of how one's childhood can impact the rest of their life.

For many years when I returned to my home state of Alabama, I would sit on the edge of my chair in restaurants. I always had the feeling that I did not belong there, and this was a direct result of racial scars from childhood.

While at a fitness center, I met a black air force veteran who confided in me. He was born and raised in Mississippi, and he stated that he read on a third grade level when he graduated from high school. Adults in his life had told him that he could not learn, and this scarred him for life.

As I reflect on my own life, I also reflect on the lives of such people as James Brown, Sam Cooke, the O'Jays, Earth Wind and Fire, the Temptations, Jackie Wilson, the Whispers, Roberta Flack, Nancy Wilson, Sammy Davis Jr., and many more. These great entertainers were at times not permitted to stay at certain hotels, eat in certain restaurants, receive limousine services, and many times could not sleep at the hotels in which they were entertaining. All of these people paved the way for the rappers and the hip-hoppers, and I hope that they truly appreciate the supreme sacrifices that were made.

Why we do what we do has always been very intriguing to me, and I always had a thirst to study human behavior. When I took my first course in general psychology, I surprisingly received an A, and the professor came up to me at the end of the semester and said, "Maybe one day we can work together as partners." At that very moment, I knew that psychology would be my field of study.

I was further motivated when a psychology professor at the University of Wisconsin-Milwaukee said to me, "If you don't get your doctorate in psychology, I'm going to come looking for you."

All of the professors at the University of Wisconsin were not that encouraging. One professor stated to the class, "Some people come back to school just to use their VA (Veterans Affairs) benefits." The professor and I had talked earlier, and he knew that I was a veteran and the only veteran in the class. I somewhat ignored his remarks, but I committed them to memory. I later took a five-credit course in neurological assessment, and I was the only male in the class and not that it mattered to me, but I felt that the teaching assistant had some questions about what I did outside of class. I carried a pager, and this was an era where very few people had pagers other than medical personnel, a few other people, and drug dealers. At that time, I also worked as a cardiovascular perfusionist for a heart surgeon, and I needed a pager. It struck me as being very odd that the teaching assistant would ask me if she could use my notebook that I kept my notes in. I did give her my notebook, and she didn't return it until the next class. During class, my pager had gone off several times, but there were messages that I needed to get from the surgeon's secretary concerning the surgical schedule. This was also the time before cell phones were in use. Because of all of the stereotypes that I encountered in other areas, I felt that the teaching assistant may have felt that by looking through my notebook, she may have been able to find out if I was indeed making a drug transaction. She may have also felt that her life and the lives of the other students may have been in jeopardy if I was indeed a drug dealer. The other reason that she took my folder could have been that since neuro assessment was a high-level course, she could have been wondering if I really comprehended the material. What she did only strengthened my resolve, and I did finish the course with a very good grade.

When I entered graduate school for clinical psychology, I drove from Milwaukee to Rolling Meadows and Chicago, Illinois, three days a week. The commute was about 110 miles one way, and many days I left Milwaukee at 7:00 a.m. and returned to Milwaukee at 11:00 p.m. My last class was generally over at 9:00 p.m., and interestingly I was never tired when I arrived at my home because I was always pumped up and full of adrenaline. This adrenaline rush was necessary because after driving the 110 miles from school, I would almost always sit at my desk and keep studying through the night. The first day of class when I drove from Milwaukee to Chicago was very strange for me. I felt very disjointed and fragmented in that half of me was in Milwaukee and the other half was in Illinois. I felt that I was shedding the old "self" and putting on a new "self." Because of this new undertaking, I knew that my life would be forever changed.

Many of my colleagues and friends thought that I was biting off more than I could chew, so to speak. I knew in my heart that I would not fail, and I also knew that I wasn't doing this alone and that I had a mission to carry out. One of my coworkers whose cup was forever half empty wanted to know how I finished my undergraduate degree so fast. What he didn't know was that I already had close to one hundred credits completed when I returned back to school to complete my degree. This person was not satisfied until he actually saw my name on the commencement program. When I was driving back and forth to Chicago to school, this same person questioned my resolve. He was sure that I would be involved in an automobile accident because of being tired. I drove back and forth from Milwaukee to Chicago in sleet, fog, rain, ice, and snow, and I always got to class on time and never missed a day at my therapy and diagnostic practicum sites, which span a period of two years. By the time I was ready to go on my internship site, I had driven back and forth from Milwaukee to Chicago three days a week for five years.

Attending the Illinois School of Professional Psychology was rigorous, challenging, stressful, and at the same time, exciting. It was, however, disheartening to discover that many of the personality theorists held racist beliefs. Oftentimes I questioned whether black people were included in all of the studies and all of the data. All too often, in many of my classes, blacks were always depicted as being at the bottom of the pile in almost everything. Today we live in a multicultural society, and it is important for this multicultural perspective to start in the classroom.

In one of my classes, the professor told the entire class that if anyone wanted to be shown the techniques of studying for tests, to see her after class. I saw her after class, and as she started to show me these techniques, she stopped abruptly and asked, "I assume you can read?" I was speechless and completely taken aback by her question. Later, I found myself becoming an overachiever in her class just to show her what I was really equipped with. I did receive As in all of her classes. Teachers, parents, and other adults have to remember that these are the types of negative perceptions that cause students to shut down academically and sometimes emotionally.

Sometimes some of my professors would also be insensitive about racial issues. In one class, we talked about testing bias when working with black and Hispanic clients, and the professor's comment was, "It would be a lot easier if everybody was the same color." We do live in a multicultural world, and you would think that a psychologist would be the first person to accept this.

In almost all of my classes, I was the only black student, and in one of these classes, someone brought up something about Hispanics and the professor said to the all-white class, "Hispanics are more like us." In my mind, he was saying that he was willing to accept Hispanics as equals but not blacks.

I did my diagnostic practicum at a clinic on the south side of Chicago (Englewood). This area also had the highest homicide rate in the entire Chicago area, and this is where I gained a vast amount of experience. I also gained a vast amount of experience working with the most impoverished population in Chicago.

During my therapy practicum, I worked at a coed adolescent correctional facility northwest of Chicago. I gained a great deal of knowledge working with adolescent males from all parts of Illinois.

However, it took some time before I was treated with respect and dignity by my supervising psychologist and a supervising social worker. The two of them were bent on breaking me down, but it didn't work. Instead of having me do a drug test in Milwaukee, which was a condition for employment, they sent me to an adult prison in Joliet, Illinois (several hours away), to give a simple urine sample. In retrospect, I think that they were doing everything they could to work my nerves.

The supervising psychologist called me into his office one day and told me that I was going to be running a group. The group consisted of twelve boys with different beliefs and value systems. Four of the boys were gang members with different affiliations, and there was also a skinhead, a KKK member, and a devil worshipper. The group was to have run for twelve weeks, but all of the boys got along so well until we ended up extending the group another eight weeks. I'm sure my supervisor was trying to scare the hell out of me, and he did not expect me to succeed. At the end of the twenty weeks, we had a pizza party for the boys, and they all got along and learned a lot from each other. Additionally, they extended warm handshakes to each other, and my heart was warmed from the entire process.

When I first arrived at the facility, everyone was talking about a female inmate who was oppositional, defiant, resistive, disruptive, and totally out of control. This inmate was in a confined area, and I asked if I could see her. When I walked on to the unit, this inmate was walking in circles on a steel table, and she was cursing me out up and down. She acted as if she didn't care what I was saying as I introduced myself and explained my role to her. She reminded me of the young girl in the movie *The Exorcist*, and you could tell that her actions could be volatile and unpredictable. Something else that struck me about this young girl was that she was disheveled and her hair was uncombed.

The next week I spent more time with her, and up to this point, she had not been attending school and no one could reach her. After meeting with her for two or three sessions, she started coming down to the main building to meet with me for her sessions. The entire institution was shocked and astonished that this young girl was attending school, behaving, maintaining her hygiene, keeping her hair neat and groomed, and getting good grades. Everyone wanted to know what I did to change her behavior, but I don't know if I did anything other than show her unconditional positive regard.

After finishing two practicums, it was time to move on to my internship site. This is a time that can be quite stressful for prospective internship students because everyone is hoping to get their number one pick also. The paperwork and the entire process can be quite stressful. I received a call from Cook County Jail in Chicago, and they were offering me a spot there, but it did not feel right. I accepted an internship position at an adolescent correctional facility in Wisconsin instead, and this is also where I did my postdoctoral internship. There were five other interns, and we were all quite close. In fact, when we started, we were told to lean on each other when the going got tough. One of the interns also attended the same school that I attended, and our offices were next to each other.

One day I was talking to my fellow intern in her office, and the painter walked in. He was a middle-aged white male, and he asked her if she wanted her office painted, and when she asked for suggestions on what color, his comment was, "Stay away from anything dark brown." I saw this as a Freudian slip, or maybe it was deliberate. He never asked me if I wanted my room painted, and he walked into my room, looked right through me, and never said a word. The other intern had her room painted but mine never was.

As interns, we became very closely knit, and we talked about many things. We all needed each other to lean on in dealing with anxiety, uncertainty, a fear of making mistakes, and worrying about the dissertation. We were supervised by at least five different psychologists, and they were genuinely interested in our welfare and our well-being.

The weekend that I started my internship, I also ended a relationship and I had to choose as to whether or not I was going to dwell on my relationship or concentrate on my internship. Needless to say, I decided that my internship was much more important.

As interns, we had to complete twelve seminars, one weekly in Madison, Wisconsin. While riding to Madison, we often stopped off for lunch and had many deep conversations from racial injustice to personal issues. One day one of the interns joked about Amish people, and we all laughed. Afterward, I felt that we were persecuting another minority group that we did not understand. I could not help but think that as a black person, we're targeted all the time. Furthermore, as psychologists, we should be empathetic, caring, and compassionate toward all people. I have a great deal of respect and reverence for Amish people, and I thought to myself that more people should practice such humility.

Being an intern brought with it many responsibilities. It was important to prioritize and not procrastinate. Packing your lunch and taking your clothes out the night before were extremely important because by doing so, you could save yourself a great deal of time and stress in the morning. The evenings while at home always passed fast, and if you did not keep up with what needed to be done, you would find yourself quite stressed. We all complained to each other about our poor planning habits and not waking up on time. It was always tempting to set the snoozer three or four times.

Sometimes interns allow stress to get the best of them, and they become ill. If you're sickly at the beginning of your internship, it's possible that you'll get sicker. We all felt that we had to take care of each other. Also, our supervisors were constantly asking us how we were doing, and it certainly made me feel better just knowing that they cared. It is important to remember that when you carry around other people's problems and worries, it can become quite stressful if not handled correctly. It must also be taken into consideration that relocating can be stressful for an intern. The intern is oftentimes leaving behind a strong support network, which may include family, friends, clients, other therapists, and supervisors. There can also be multiple intervening variables that come into play at the internship site that can add to the already heightened anxiety.

During an internship, support is critical and it should not just come from supervisors and fellow interns but from anyone who has direct contact with an intern. Many interns also finish their dissertations while on their internships, and this compounds their stress in many ways. Oftentimes the intern may have to travel more than a thousand miles to defend his or her dissertation, and the oral defense can be a nightmare for some. All too often, many interns end up burned out by the time it's time to take the national boards.

Report writing can be another problem for many interns. At some sites, interns are required to produce twelve psychological evaluations before the end of their internship. Unfortunately, many interns wait until the last minute to do these, and then they're overwhelmed. My suggestion would be for the intern to do at least one and a half reports per month. The key to everything is to pace yourself. When I did my first psychological evaluation, my supervisor went over it with a fine-tooth comb, and I had to redo it three times before he accepted it. I was quite angry about this, but in the long run, I understood why he was doing what he was doing. My ability to construct a sound and accurate psychological evaluation was greatly enhanced because of his time and attention to detail.

Also, during your internship, what can happen, will happen. Financially, I was struggling, and my engine went out in my car, which cost me three thousand dollars. I was given a loaner car, and that week it was my turn to drive to Madison with the other interns to attend our weekly seminar. One of the male interns asked, "Why didn't you ask for a Cadillac?" My response was, "I don't like Cadillacs." Again, this was a stereotype.

I also had two root canals done and an extraction. I had dental bills at three dentists' offices and was unable to pay all three bills in full, but they kept calling me. It was also a while before I could get medical insurance coverage.

At that time I was spending about twenty dollars a week on food, and when I called the phone company to make arrangements to pay a seventy-five-dollar phone bill, the lady who took the call was very arrogant in saying, "How did your bill get so high?" When you're an intern, luxury is not something that is important to you, and you become accustomed to struggling and living near the poverty line, and this also is something that keeps you motivated because you know that one day, your hard work will pay off. As my father always said, "There is a light at the end of the tunnel."

During the internship, I also applied for many part-time jobs and got them. I worked for a company called Clean Power but only worked one evening because I had a reaction to one of the cleaning agents. Later, I was hired as a limousine driver, and our job was to transport passengers to and from the airport. The driver who trained me was a middle-aged man who talked incessantly. One night we picked up three flight attendants from a hotel and transported them to Mitchell International Airport. One of the female flight attendants, for some reason, started talking about locking up criminals and throwing away the keys because they'd never be rehabilitated. Needless to say, she did not know that I was doing an internship in psychology at a correctional facility. Being my usual self, I listened without saying a word in response.

The driver who was training me was going through a divorce, and he was quite angry at his ex-wife. He accused her of trying to destroy him and hurt him by taking his son away. His comments reminded me of my own divorce, except the anger and the pain of my divorce were gone. I did not like driving the limousine, and I tried something else.

The next job I landed was as a material handler at a major department store where I was making seven dollars per hour. For some reason the concrete floor in the plant was quite hard and very uncomfortable on my feet. This job lasted for one night.

Finally, I accepted a job that was suitable. This job entailed delivering the *Milwaukee Journal Sentinel* newspaper. This was a seven-days-a-week job whereby my route started at about 2:00 a.m. and I was done around 5:00 a.m. There were about one hundred customers on my route and more on Sundays. The Sunday papers were also heavier and thicker, and this gave me quite a workout. This job also lasted for several months, and it paid roughly 210 dollars per week. Many of the paper carriers like me were struggling to make ends meet. Most of them were grouchy and almost never spoke to each other.

My paper route was in the heart of the central city in a high crime area, and safety was not a big concern for me. Prostitutes also frequented this area, and on one particular night, a prostitute walked up to my car and said, "Throw those newspapers in the back seat, this will only take five minutes." My response to her was, "I don't have five minutes," and as I sped off, she started cursing me out.

On another occasion at 4:00 a.m., three teenage boys had just stolen a car ran in front of my car, and a few minutes later, I saw a police cruiser and I stopped them to give a description and a direction that the teenagers had gone. Inside the police car were a white male officer and a white female officer. As I was trying to assist the officers, the white male officer never looked at me, but the female officer smiled and was attentive. The white male officer probably saw me as another black male who could not be trusted, but my cooperation helped them to catch the thieves.

As interns, we were at the halfway point of a yearlong internship. The crunch was on, and we were starting to unnerve each other. Personalities were starting to clash, and the drive to Madison was starting to become stressful and strained for some of the interns. Once while in Madison at a seminar given by a well-known black psychologist, we were discussing issues pertaining to working with black clients, and my position was that Milwaukee would be a much better city if it had historical black colleges like the ones in Atlanta. It was unfortunate that one of the interns misconstrued my statement. She went back and told one of our supervisors that I was being oversensitive and derisive of Milwaukee. This intern completely missed the salient point that was intended. My supervisor then called me and accused me of being a ticking time bomb. His comment was unfair and presumptuous, and he probably should have talked to me first to get my explanation. Also, the other interns were quick to stand up for their rights and voice their strong opinions, but when I did it, I was called a rebel or a militant.

As interns, we got to know each other quite well. One of the interns shared with me the fact that a close family member was the grand dragon of the Ku Klux Klan in another state. She seemed quite embarrassed about this, but she also needed to vent about it. Over 80 percent of the clients that we worked with were black, and a great percentage of the interns were not used to working with black clients. One day, one of the female white interns tested a black youth, and she stated that the youth did not know the difference between a donkey and a house. When she asked the youth what a donkey was, he responded by saying that it was "hoss." The closest thing to a donkey would have been a horse and the youth was correct, but he pronounced horse as "house" or "hoss." When the intern shared her experience with me and the other interns, no one else picked up on this very critical error. This is also an example of the importance of cultural sensitivity.

On Labor Day weekend, 1996, I finished my predoctoral internship. That weekend was supposed to have been quiet and relaxing, but instead, that Saturday morning, my mother called and informed me that my maternal grandmother had died. That morning it was sunny and clear, and there was no reason for all of the electricity in the house to shut off, but as soon as the phone rang (my mother's phone call), everything shut off.

Many people do not understand the process of becoming a clinical psychologist. Day after day, many people would ask the same question, "Are you done yet?" Other people would ask, "Are you going to finish school before you retire?" In becoming a clinical psychologist, one has to complete 120 credits, a one year therapy practicum, a one year diagnostic practicum, a comprehensive examination, a one year predoctoral internship, a one year postdoctoral internship, completion of a dissertation and oral defense of the dissertation, a National Board examination, and a State Ethics examination. One has to remember that usually what can happen, will happen. One's anxiety level can increase from many things. At the end of my postdoctoral internship, I went to my dentist expecting to get my teeth cleaned, but upon entering the exam room, I noticed that they had a tray of surgical instruments laid out, and my comment was, "But I am just having a cleaning done today." The technician answered swiftly, "No, the dentist is pulling your wisdom tooth today."

The next week it was time for the dreaded annual physical, and lying on the table in the doctor's exam room was a tube of KY jelly and a pair of latex gloves, which meant the prostate exam was on his list of things to do. While experiencing this medical trauma, if you will, I was also getting ready to take the ethics exam and being interviewed by the examining board.

While going through the process of becoming a psychologist, it is important to practice your faith if you believe in a supreme being. As a graduate student, it was not embarrassing to me to fall to my knees on a regular basis and pray for guidance and direction.

Church attendance on a regular basis was also important for me. People still look at me funny when I tell them that I am Catholic, and this look comes mostly from other blacks. Many black people who are not Catholic believe that there's no preaching in the Catholic religion. One of my clients was talking to another family member about Moses receiving the Commandments from God, and she looked at me and said, "Being Catholic, you don't know anything about that because Catholics don't preach." Without a hesitation, my comment was, "Yes, we do." If a black person is not a democrat, he or she is criticized by other blacks, but people should be able to choose whatever party or whatever religion they desire. I contemplated becoming Catholic at age seventeen and became Catholic at age eighteen. Many of my clients have had a strong reaction to my being Catholic, and for that reason it's not wise to discuss religion. Many of my clients will ask, "How long have you been Catholic?" Another client asked if Catholics prayed to Mary and why do we make the sign of the cross. After that question, he also started laughing. People choose whatever religion they want to be, and we should never demean anyone or anyone's religion. The question that I detest most is, "Why are you Catholic?" I would never ask anyone why they're Mormon, Jehovah's Witness, Baptist, Methodist, Muslim, Lutheran, or anything else. We all have free will, and no one is going to dictate to me what religion is right for me.

Even though blacks have not always been accepted fully into the Catholic church, there are millions of black Catholics on the continent of Africa and in the United States. In the 1980s, I attended a Catholic church in Milwaukee and was not a member but attended regularly. After meeting with the priest and telling him that I was not a member, I did not expect him to include this in his homily the following week. What he said was, "If you're not a member, we don't need you." After thinking it through, I moved to All Saints Catholic Church, where I have been quite content. Also, the congregation is around 80 percent black. It did take some time before settling in. When my children were younger, I wanted to enroll them in a Catholic school on the east side of Milwaukee, and when I approached the building, the janitor would not talk to me and the teacher locked her door when she saw me coming down the hallway. At that point, it would have been easy to give up on Catholicism, but God is in the sacraments, the prayers, and the teachings of the church. As was stated fervently in the 1960s, "Ain't gonna let nobody turn me around." To leave the Catholic church would be an insult to the black pioneers such as Daniel Rudd, Elizabeth Lange, Pierre Toussaint, and many others who helped to build the church. Yes, the Catholic church has sinned, but each week at mass we hear, "This is the lamb of God who takes away the sins of the world. Happy are those who are called to his supper." Our response is, "Lord, I am not worthy to receive you but only say the word and I shall be healed."

After receiving my doctorate degree, a Caucasian man walked up to me and said, "This must have been really tough for you."

Upon starting to practice psychology, I started to learn many more things about human nature. I remember driving my car to an apartment complex to see a client, and upon arriving at the complex it was roped off, causing me to have to park across the street. The landlord who was white happened to come into the same house that I was visiting and stated, "There's a Jaguar parked across the street. It must belong to a drug dealer." My client immediately stated, "No, that's Dr. Bracy's car." The landlord then looked at me and dropped his head in embarrassment.

My old neighborhood around North Fortieth Street and Villard Avenue sizzled with much activity. One night I stopped at a popular convenience store one block from my home, and upon entering the store, two middle-aged black men were talking to each other and they wanted to know how much did my Jaguar cost, and upon giving them a response, one of them replied, "That's a lot of money." The other one quickly chimed in and stated, "He must be rich," and his friend quickly said, "No, he has all these girls around here taking care of him." My response then was, "No, I've worked hard to get what I have."

This is also an example of a double negative, which means that you're looked at negatively with two sets of lenses, one black and one white. White people will stereotype black people without having any sound basis for it, and black people do the same thing to other blacks without any justification.

Believe it or not, these types of incidents happened all the time. One morning at 7:00 a.m., I rushed out of my house to go and get a haircut. Upon backing out of my driveway, I noticed a black Blazer parked across the street, but seeing unidentified parked cars across the street was not unusual. Upon arriving back, I noticed two police officers walking around the Blazer, but I wasn't too concerned because it was commonplace to see police officers all over the neighborhood. I exited my car and ran into my house to take a shower before seeing clients all day. Rushing from my car to my house was something that was done all the time because being punctual for my therapy sessions with my clients was important to me. Approximately two minutes after entering my home, the doorbell rang and it was the black police officer. He informed me that the Blazer was stolen and guns were involved. I cooperated fully by giving him my name, telephone number, and age as he requested. I also told him that I had not seen anything unusual and he left. Two minutes later, his white partner knocked on the door, and upon opening the door his first comment was, "My partner said that from your body language, you know something about that Blazer." My response was, "Tell your partner that I'm a clinical psychologist, and his assessment is all wrong. I then gave him by business card, closed the door, and continued getting ready for my long day of seeing clients. What happened to me only reinforces the notion that oftentimes being black can mean that you're guilty until proven innocent.

One of my black female clients was guilty until proven innocent, but it took her to die before this was discovered. Her story is as follows:

I worked with a forty-four-year-old woman who felt that she was the black sheep of the family. She had a history of drug abuse and had lost custody of her children. Three of the children were returned to her and were living with her while I worked with the family. This lady suffered from asthma, emphysema, diabetes, heart disease, hypertension, back problems, and she was probably going to need a total knee replacement. While working with the client, she struggled emotionally, physically, and financially. In spite of the misery in her life, she also managed to smile whenever I met with her. This client also needed oxygen to assist her breathing, and one week when I met with her, she expressed a desire to change the time and the day that I met with her. She wanted to meet with me on Monday instead of Thursday. I did accommodate her, and I met with her on Monday night. Her electricity had been turned off for nonpayment of her bill, and it was cold inside her flat. She was pulling electricity from the downstairs unit, and there was a space heater in the living room. She also had a mattress in the middle of the living room floor because she may have been more comfortable there. She had been sleeping in her bedroom, but it may have been too cold and too secluded for her. Her three teenagers (two boys and one girl) were not at home, and this appeared to have bothered her.

    During this session, her hair looked really shiny, and she smiled, laughed, and joked more than she had ever done. She also talked about being denied Social Security benefits. Even though her phone and electricity were turned off, she seemed at peace. At times she would talk about her biblical beliefs. She also thanked me for changing the time and date of seeing her. When this client spoke with me, she talked about wanting to see her children who had been adopted, and she talked about how much she loved them. She also talked about her three children who lived with her and what she wanted for each one of them. She described their personal nuances and their personalities with precision. After the session was over, she shook my hand, and for some reason, an eerie feeling came over me as I walked to my car. The next day when her son came home from school, he found her on the mattress in the living room, dead. It was unfortunate that one son went to Corrections and one son was eventually sent to Children's Detention. The system not only failed her, but it failed her sons as well. Someone should have stepped in with an umbrella and a safety net rather than being punitive. Because of all her medical problems, her lights and gas should not have been turned off.

After her death, a close family member informed the Medical Examiner's office and the newsroom that she was on drugs, and the reason she had her utilities turned off was because she was using Social Security money for drugs. I was the last person to talk with her other than her children, and I did not believe that she was doing drugs. Her apartment was not much, but she did keep it clean and I felt that she had a legitimate reason for having the mattress on the living room floor. A news reporter reported to me that dishes were piled in the sink and an ashtray was overflowing with cigarette butts. It was my impression that this lady had given up all hope of having a good life and being happy. I also feel that she had slipped into a severe depression. I called the Medical Examiner's office several times to get the autopsy report, and after much persistence I did finally receive it. The autopsy report stated that there were no drugs in her system and that she died of heart disease brought on by hypertension. The television station refused to do a story on her because they saw her as being a drug addict. Even after receiving the autopsy report, they still would not do a story. As mental health workers, it is important to advocate for our clients, and it is even more important to advocate when they have no voice. As the psychologist for this family, I will continue to tell this story over and over and over again. Through the autopsy report, her name was cleared, but I'm not ready to put it to rest yet. I think that there was a reason that I was able to spend an hour and a half with her the night before she died. I truly feel that she wanted me to continue to tell this story.

People can die from hopelessness and depression. During the space shuttle missions in the 1960s and 1970s, every time NASA had a successful launch, they would fire some of their aeronautical engineers, and upon being fired, these engineers exhibited some of the same signs that we see in marginalized people. These engineers were suffering from alcohol abuse, drug abuse, depression, divorce, hopelessness, and heart attacks.

Upon autopsying the engineers, it was found that there was a rush of adrenaline into the bloodstream that spilled into the myocardial tissue of the heart, which caused massive heart attacks. This was a stress response from depression, anxiety, helplessness, and hopelessness. When we're dealing with any client, we have to understand all of the dynamics that come into play. There are many people who live this on a daily basis. We do live in the richest country in the world, and the rest of the world continues to look to us for guidance and direction. As far as we know, Native Americans were the first inhabitants of the United States. The rest of us came across the Atlantic Ocean, some freely and some of us in bondage. Even in 2008, the slave deficit theory is still held by some people in medicine and psychology.

Recently, I attended a lecture at Marquette University, presented by a well-known black priest who spoke on racism in religion, and during the discussion period, a retired professor from Marquette stood up and said that he grew up in the Irish ghetto in Brooklyn, and when he was a kid, he and his family would oftentimes degrade the coloreds. He went on to say that in his adult life, he went out of his way to help minorities. He wondered if it had something to do with his own guilt as he enters the twilight years of his life. We are one people, and as Martin Luther King so eloquently stated, "We're bound together in a mutual destiny."

As a black clinical psychologist, I have encountered many situations where people wondered if I was a real doctor or even sometimes if I was old enough to be a doctor. Sometimes, all black social service agencies will need expert consultation, but they may expect me to consult for nothing or a nominal fee but will bring in a white consultant for whatever price is requested. Many people will accept my expertise, but there are others who choose to dismiss it. As a black psychologist working closely with black children and black families, my knowledge base is vast and many people tend to overlook this reality. Many mental health workers have a tendency to want to dominate meetings and come across as being the real expert. When attending meetings or working with anyone, it is important to listen, analyze, assess, and observe. For many people, they choose to talk all the time, and they never cue in to crucial environmental stimuli.

There are also very few doctorate-level clinical psychologists who do in-home therapy, and being a rarity, people tend to take you for granted. Many professional people tend not to respect my schedule, and when scheduling family meetings, I may not always get the same consideration that a white psychologist would get. Some families will also undermine the work that you do and will find ways to diminish your worth. As a black psychologist, some families will know that I'm doing a good job but will refuse to admit it because I am a black man and how am I supposed to have all that knowledge. Some families also have a tendency to split teams to serve their own agenda.

On one occasion, I was about to start a stress and coping seminar for high school students attending a suburban school outside of Milwaukee. All of these students were white, and as I was about to start, a white male teacher started running from the back of the room, and he was coming toward me at a rapid speed. As he approached me, he stated, "These are not Chapter 220 kids," which meant that they were not bussed and his real unspoken question to me was, "Why are you, a black man, talking to these white suburban kids about coping." Likewise, people do not want President Barack Obama talking to their children about education. They attempted to shut me down because I was talking about stress and coping from a black person's perspective.

One spring afternoon, I was in Children's Court, and my hope was that the judge would release my adolescent client to a shelter rather than keep him in detention. The judge chose to keep my client in detention, in spite of the attorney's strong defense to release him. As I talked to my client's attorney and another professional person, who was black, the attorney said to the professional, "I was disappointed with the outcome today, but we have Dr. Bracy on the case, he can help us the next time we go to court." The professional then laughed, and from the tone of her voice, she sounded as if she knew the attorney and I were in agreement, but she still didn't seem to value my professional input. I felt diminished, and after talking with the family later on, I discovered that I was not paranoid because an observant adult relative of my client detected what I had detected coming from the professional. In fact, the family member came to me and said, "I don't like the way she treated you." He felt that she deliberately disrespected me as a psychologist. This happens quite often in everyday life, and it is another example of the double negative that I refer to often.

On another occasion, I waited outside of court for approximately four hours. When our case was finally called in, the judge walked past us as he positioned himself in his seat. A black social worker and I were sitting in the back row in the courtroom along with a family member. He then stood up from his chair and glared at us and started reprimanding us about not being good parents. He continued on his tirade about if we were better parents, we wouldn't have to deal with all of these problems. It was obvious that he saw black faces in the back of the court room, and he assumed that we had to have been there for our children. As a psychologist, I wanted to go home just like he wanted to go home, and the hours I put in each day were probably longer than what he put in. Even in 2010, black people should not rest on their laurels because they have acquired several degrees. Stereotypes continue to permeate society, and like it or not, we must remain forever vigilant.

The double negative shows its ugly face again when black people tell you that they're not going to see a psychologist because they're not crazy. Also, in some instances, a family member is ostracized and ridiculed because they're seeing a psychologist. Other people might say, "If you're a psychologist, does that mean that you're reading my mind?" Unfortunately, many people run from therapy rather than embrace it. My position is that if people take advantage of psychotherapy, they will fare much better in many areas of their lives.

Finally, being a black psychologist carries with it a great deal of responsibility, stress, and anxiety. It is also important to deal with stress in a positive manner.

When I was done with everything except my licensing exam, I traveled to Alabama at Christmastime.

Christmas Eve, I was sitting at the kitchen table having breakfast with my father, and I remember having two strong cups of coffee and I had taken a Tagamet the night before, and I took one while having breakfast, which was a mistake because I found out later that I should have only taken one in a twenty-four-hour period. I found out later that I may have had an adverse reaction to Tagamet, but more important than that, I think I came close to death. I was shopping at Dillard's when I felt like my body was shutting down. The sensation was like a furnace shutting completely down, and at that moment I felt that I had no control at all. My entire face felt cold, numb, and I felt a sense of doom as if I was dying. The only thing that I could do was drop to my knees, and I felt that I would lose consciousness at any moment. I kept telling God, "Please not here." If I was going to die, I wanted it to be at home with my family.

Being previously in the medical field, the only thing that came to me was to take some deep breaths, slowly. I did this and I felt that I was still in distress, but I was hanging on. I felt weak, confused, and I could hear and feel my heart pounding at a rapid rate, and this was frightening because it had never happened before. I managed to drive myself to my parent's home, but I knew that something was not right. When I walked into the house, everyone was in a jovial mood, and they were expecting me to reciprocate. As I walked throughout the house, family members were speaking to me and being joyous, and I was pretending to be in the Christmas spirit. As I walked about the house, the rooms were spinning but I did not want to alarm anyone.

My friend Wanda was with me, and I said to her embarrassingly, we need to go for a ride. My intent was to go to the emergency room without telling anyone. The hospital was less than a mile away, and Wanda was under the impression that I needed some type of X-ray taken. When we walked into the emergency room, I saw one of my old teachers, but because of my confusion, I called her by a different name. I gave the nurse my symptoms, and as she was talking to me, she was taking my blood pressure. I knew that something was not right, and I was expecting the worst. After taking my blood pressure, the nurse ripped the cuff off of my arm, grabbed me by my arm, and started running with me and screaming out stat orders. My blood pressure was 230/120, which meant I was nearing a stroke or a heart attack.

My friend Wanda then called my parents, and my mother dealt with her fear by staying away from the hospital, and my father was there in five minutes. As he sat next to my bed, I knew that he had been praying all the way there, and he was still praying. The doctor came in, and he talked to me and did his routine examination and everything checked out. Even though I had been tachycardic (rapid heart rate), my EKG was stabilizing and my blood pressure was stabilizing without any type of intervention. As the physician talked to me, I was hooked up to a continuous monitor that gave a constant read out of my blood pressure. The attending physician was a white male with a strong southern accent, but this time his accent did not bother me; in fact, it was soothing. He had great bedside manners, and he had done a rotation at one of the hospitals in Milwaukee where I had worked as a cardiovascular perfusionist. As I laid there talking and relaxing, my blood pressure came down to 132/82, and the emergency room physician released me. Even though my blood pressure came back to normal, I felt that my body had been attacked and I had come close to death. I can truly say that I think I know what it feels like to die suddenly.

With me, I wanted to return to Milwaukee to finish my unfinished business. It was also important to me to be able to see my son and daughter in Milwaukee. This experience reminded me that we have no control over the inner workings of our bodies, and we don't choose the place or the time where we die. We must all keep in mind that our loved ones can leave home expecting to return and not return. We all must work harder at being kinder and gentler to each other and don't be afraid to say I love you.

Upon my return to Milwaukee, I still felt that my body had been insulted, and I made an appointment with my personal physician, and at that time, my blood pressure was fine. He also did a brain scan, ordered a stress test, and a multitude of blood gases. Everything that he ordered came back negative, but I still wasn't feeling like myself. The emergency room physician in Alabama diagnosed my condition as a stress response, and in my mind, it could have been a culmination of the entire process of graduate school. Graduate students have to be careful not to burn themselves out and end up experiencing anxiety, depression, or other disorders at the end of their training.

As I continue to do my work in helping humankind, I would like to do it to the best of my abilities. We all have a responsibility to lay the groundwork to enhance the welfare of generations to come.

As Saint Francis of Assisi said, "I have done what is mine to do, may God teach you yours."

Like Saint Francis of Assisi, my life, my mission, and my deeds will be perpetuated through my descendants and others as they improve, not only their lives but the lives of others. Through the help of God, may the flames of justice and love permeate the universe and hatred and bitterness be extinguished.

The first home that I purchased after leaving the military

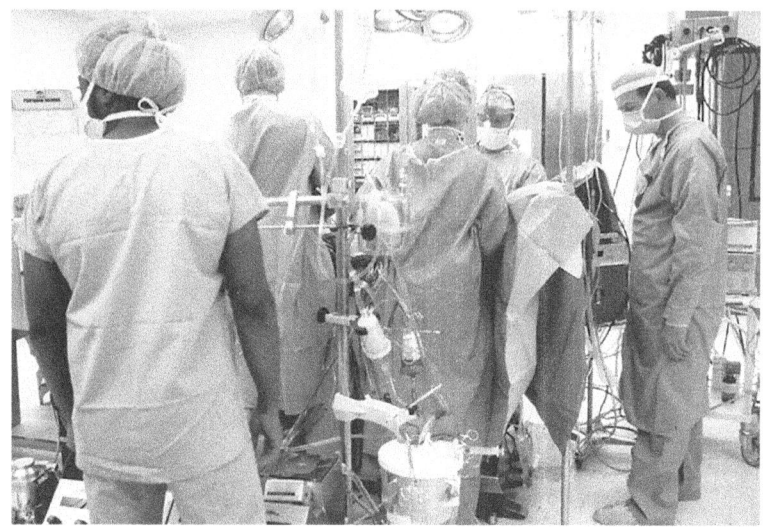

A picture of me operating the heart-lung machine prior to putting the patient on total cardiopulmonary bypass. The surgeon facing me with the headlamp on is heart surgeon, Dr. Richard T. Shore.

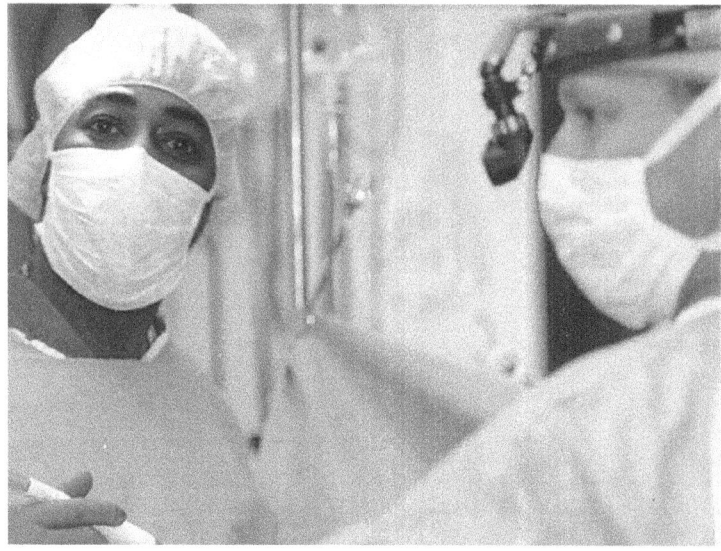

One of my other duties was to assist Dr. Shore in opening and closing the patient. I am standing across from him at the operating room table during an open-heart procedure.

Uncle Claude, whom I spent many weekends
with as a boy in Milwaukee

My sister Joyce is sitting in the middle between my mother
and grandmother. Joyce's grandson is in front of her.

My uncle Wilmer who I lived with in Oak Creek, Wisconsin

With my employer Dr. Richard T. Shore, a gifted heart surgeon

Samantha Webb Dortch
1905 - 1997

My grandmother Samantha Webb-Dortch actually died one day after finishing my internship.

An earlier picture of my grandmother

Neighborhood where my children grew up (with son Earl Jr.)

My daughter and her husband, Kevin, who live in Alabama

CHAPTER SEVEN

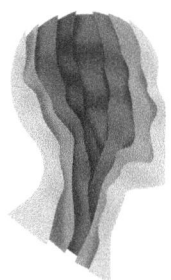

My Personal Grief (The Untimely Death of My Daughter)

When many parents think of death, they think in terms of the natural order of things, which generally means that the parent will die before the child. When the opposite happens, it can incapacitate and immobilize an already grieving parent.

As a psychologist, I thought long and intensely about who I wanted to have as a secretary. My daughter, Yolanda, had worked as a unit clerk at the VA Hospital, St. Joseph's in Milwaukee, and she worked for Blue Cross and Blue Shield. I decided to give her a chance at working as my secretary, and she kept this position from 2002 to 2005. She always felt like she had to protect her father, and she did an excellent job of keeping things orderly and neat. If I needed office supplies and I gave her a one hundred dollar bill to purchase ninety-nine dollars and seventy-six cents worth of supplies, she would purchase the supplies, and she would always make sure that the receipt and the change of twenty-four cents, or whatever it was, was left on my desk.

Yolanda was the firstborn, and she had an inquisitiveness about her concerning everything. As a little girl and as an adult, Yolanda was outspoken, sensitive, opinionated, and defiant at times. If I had to pick who the protector was in the family, I would say that it was Yolanda. Even though I am the psychologist, she didn't like it if she felt like someone was taking advantage of her father, and she would let it be known in not such a gentle manner.

The last day that Yolanda worked at my office was Thursday, July 28, 2005. Her demeanor was a little different, but this was not unusual for her. During the spring of that year, I specifically remember her telling me, "Daddy, when I die, I want to be cremated." I remember chuckling and not taking her serious. Sometimes she would make off the wall comments, and I felt like this was another one of her spontaneous and outrageous comments. As I jokingly questioned her about her statement, she further stated, "I really don't think that I am going to live very long." As a father, I questioned her about this, but she didn't give me very much information so I did not pursue it any further. Because Yolanda was so outspoken and opinionated, I simply felt that she was trying to get a reaction. At that time, her relationship with her boyfriend was not the greatest, and I was accustomed to her varying moods because of the turmoil in her relationship.

I remember going to sleep Saturday night, July 30, 2005 and having a very strange dream. I dreamt that the priest from my parish, Father Carl Diederichs, was sprinkling incense at mass during Christmastime. Another pastor from my sister's church in Alabama, Pastor Henry Crawford, who was my classmate in high school, was also in the dream. As the dream unfolded, Father Carl jumped into the arms of Pastor Henry Crawford. The dream itself could have coincided with the actual time of Yolanda's death. I truly believe that when the car accident occurred, psychically, I was tapping into it in my sleep. Before going any further, let me say that my daughter Yolanda and her boyfriend were killed in an automobile accident. Her boyfriend was driving the car and hit a tree at eighty-five miles per hour. To this day, I still have my doubts as to whether this was an accident or a deliberate homicide. It hasn't been revealed to me yet, but I feel that one day it will be.

The dream that I had the night of Yolanda's death was significant because in the dream, Father Carl and Pastor Henry Crawford appeared, and in real life, Father Carl officiated at Yolanda's funeral and Pastor Henry Crawford was the first person to send a sympathy card from Alabama. Father Carl also went through the ritual of incensing her draped coffin, and this was the meaning of the incense in my dream.

On Sunday morning, July 31, 2005, I woke up and nothing seemed unusual. I was in the habit of walking every morning, and the morning of July 31 was no different. I prayed as I walked, and I prayed for all family members, and this is something that I did routinely. That day I became angry at God, and I stopped praying for quite some time. I walked north on Ninety-First Street at about 8:30 a.m., and I had no idea that sometime earlier that night, my daughter and her boyfriend had been killed on Ninety-First Street approximately one mile from my home. Sirens usually woke me up at night, especially if a police car or an ambulance was traveling on Ninety-First Street. On that fateful night, I did not hear any sirens at all. However, it's possible that I may have been so busy dreaming that night until all other external stimuli was blocked out.

After my walk, I returned back to my home at about 9:30 a.m. Before I could get settled in, the phone rang and it was my niece, Angela, calling. The first question she asked me was, "Uncle Earl, do you know where Yolanda is?" I remember my first verbal response being no, but in a very weak voice, I sensed that something was wrong and I was thinking to myself that maybe she was involved in an accident but she was OK or maybe she had been arrested for something. Angela went on to tell me that she had a friend who worked at the medical examiner's office (the morgue), and they had brought a Yolanda Bracy in along with a male companion. I did not recognize the name of the male companion (her boyfriend) because Yolanda always used his nickname.

The feeling in the pit of my stomach that I felt that morning and the buckling of my knees, I would not wish on anyone. I felt like a boxer being hit to the chin with a powerful left hook and a combination with the right hand going to the abdomen. I felt my body shutting down, and I felt my strong and manly voice disappearing. I was hearing my niece, but at the same time, I felt vulnerable, weak, and childlike. Being the uncle, I was supposed to be giving instructions, but she was and I felt powerless because I could barely talk. A feeling of numbness fell over my body, and I immediately lost my appetite. It is very interesting how the body reacts to being traumatized. I immediately became very hyperactive, and I could not stop pacing.

I spent all day Sunday pacing and talking to relatives on the phone. They all were consoling me, but I talked very little because to talk meant that I would lose my composure. I even remember pinching myself and saying, "This has got to be a dream. I have to wake up soon."

I did not attend mass that Sunday morning but instead, I was walking around in a daze all day. I now know how the people in Haiti felt when the earthquake struck. If it looked like they were walking around like zombies, it's because they felt like zombies. When a person is in a state of confusion and the mind is blinded by turbulence, there is also a certain amount of catatonia that sets in, and the body shifts into a slow-motion mode.

On Sunday morning, July 31, 2005, as time passed slowly, I called my ex-wife (Olivia), Yolanda's mother, and I told her what was told to me by my niece, Angela. I tried to break the news gently to her, and I could hear the denial in her voice. She asked me if I had called Yolanda's cell phone, and later on I did call it but there was no answer. I guess I was in denial as well, and maybe I was expecting a miracle. Being in separate households, I'm not sure how my ex-wife dealt with her grief and pain that day, but I have a feeling that she wanted to die as well.

Later that day, my numbness was turning to anger. I was angry at Yolanda's boyfriend for being reckless and irresponsible, and I found myself becoming angry at Yolanda for allowing him to drive her car. Being a psychologist, trained in grief issues, I also knew that I had to be there for the rest of the family. My body then shifted into a survival mode. I knew that my job was to be a fortress for my ex-wife, my other two children, Earl Jr. and Sonia, and Yolanda's children.

Upon retiring to bed that Sunday evening, I thought about my schedule for the coming week. I knew that I had clients to see and funeral arrangements had to be made. Picking up the telephone to make funeral arrangements for a loved one is not an easy task, and this is why we all need the support of relatives during such a difficult time. During the coming week, in addition to planning Yolanda's funeral, I also kept my schedule with many of my clients. Interestingly, many of them did not know that my daughter had been killed because I did not share this with them. I continued my therapeutic interchange, and I tried to be as empathetic and compassionate as possible. In retrospect, I should have taken some time off for myself, but the downfall of a good psychologist is that they want to always be there for their clients.

Monday morning, August 1, 2005, one day after the accident, I called my personal physician, and I was able to see him that Monday morning. He knew from the news reports what had happened, and he checked me over thoroughly to make sure that I was OK. My personal physician's name is Dr. Michael Fetherstone, and the one thing that stood out the most about that appointment with him was that he cradled me in his arms like a baby for at least two minutes. That embrace was probably the best thing that happened to me that entire week because I found it to be sincere, nurturing, soothing, and paternalistic. Dr. Fetherstone's departing words to me were, "If you need anything, let us know."

In addition to reading about my daughter's death in the local newspaper, it was being continuously piped into my living room via the television, and I had no control over what was being said. The media does not care about sensitivity when they're reporting a death. They may say something like a twenty-six-year-old male and his female companion hit a tree at a speed of eighty-five miles per hour, and both died en route to the hospital. They don't care if the parents, the grandparents, the children, or other relatives are listening. They merely want to sensationalize the event. I remember walking out of the room several times during the news coverage of my daughter's death. If death came violently to the son or daughter of someone in the news media, maybe they would think twice about their level of insensitivity in reporting the news.

We all have to remember that anyone of us can have the rug pulled from underneath us at any time. Sometimes, other people will come across as arrogant, pompous, or they may continue to search your face for signs of distress or pain. People need to know what questions to ask and what questions not to ask. One has to remember that an unthought-out question or comment can be quite hurtful to the bereaved.

I found myself having a very strong negative reaction whenever people would stand one inch from my nose and study my face and ask me, "How are you doing?" I always got the feeling that many of them would have gotten great joy out of seeing me fall apart. During the initial grief period and beyond, do not ask a person how they're doing. Instead, say something like, "I'm glad to see you," or "You're looking well." To ask a person how they're doing, I think, sets off a chain reaction. The one thing that you do not want to do and the thing that I refused to do was grieve my life away and have a pity party.

Four years later, people still look at me funny and ask, "How are you doing?" First of all, I think that it's not sincere, and some people enjoy seeing other people hurting and miserable. I can truly say that I have moved beyond hurt and pain and I have a life to live. My life was changed forever, but we all have to adapt to change and move forward and teach what we have learned from life's lessons. The planet earth is billions of years old, and we are here for only seconds in comparison to the age of the universe. To lose a loved one does not mean that you have to roll over and die as well. My father used to say, "We did not come here to stay." Also, our loved ones don't belong to us, and we have to give them back.

Since Yolanda's death and since my father's death, I have made several trips to Holy Hill, Wisconsin, where I do my writing, contemplating, and visiting the Basilica and the fourteen Stations of the Cross. Being inhabitants of the earth is a mystery, but when you visit the Stations of the Cross, you see the suffering of Christ and you understand why he made the sacrifices that he made and to suffer on earth is part of his divine plan. I firmly believe that death is not a finality but instead a rebirth.

It is important to keep in mind that after a death of a loved one, other people will try and make you grieve. They will say such things as, "Be strong," or "I know you must be hurting." If the grieving person says, "I feel OK," the other person will try and make them feel something that they don't feel. The person who has experienced the death of a loved one does not always feel pain. Friends and acquaintances can sometimes be irritating and aggravating when they say such things as, "Are you sure you're OK?" or "I know you're hurting." The fact of the matter is they don't know this, and it is not right to assume such a thing.

A friend of mine said to me, "You're going to have a lot of days when you just want to cry." This was the farthest thing from the truth because I never had those days. This same person went on to say, "The worst is yet to come." I found this not to be true either. We all grieve in our own way and in our own time. As a psychologist, it is important for me to remember that some people can get over the death of a loved one and move on with their lives in a matter of six months to a year. On the other hand, it can take some people twenty years or a whole lifetime. My job as a psychologist is to help them to become unstuck.

I also feel that I helped my ex-wife, Olivia, through the grieving process as well. In the coming weeks after Yolanda's death, Olivia informed me that she felt as if her heart was stopping. This type of physical sequela is part of the grieving process. Sometimes people are numb during the funeral and this acts as an anesthetic, but it wears off after the funeral and this is when the pain really hits. The grief that people feel can be compared to an aftershock that people experience after an earthquake. The last earthquake that occurred in Chile was approximately 8.8 on the Richter scale, but after the major earthquake, there were 90 aftershocks, and people never knew when they were going to hit. It is the same with the aftershocks during grief. You never know when they're going to hit, or you never know when your world is going to be shaken. The residual grief continues to come unexpectedly.

During the grieving process, many people see you as being vulnerable and weak and will try and take advantage of you in many ways. Some people may feel that you're not thinking clearly, and they may feel that they have to think for you.

About a year after my daughter's death, I met a group of my peers from the medical field whom I used to work with at a restaurant in downtown Milwaukee. Many of these people I had not seen in ten to fifteen years. When I walked into the restaurant, they all looked at me in a strange manner. Since my daughter was killed, I think they expected me to walk in bent over, looking worn out, decrepit, and dejected. I also got the feeling that people did not know quite what to say. One of my ex coworkers came up to me later and said, "Earl, you look really good, you look ten years younger." I think that sometimes people expect you to have a cigarette in one hand and a glass of alcohol in the other. When you are grieving or not grieving, it is important to drink plenty of water, avoid excessive alcohol and cigarettes, get plenty of rest, rely on your faith, stay active, connect with family and friends, maintain a balanced diet, eat plenty of fruits and vegetables, take vitamins if need be, and keep your stress level in check.

I am also a person who dreams often, and as a psychologist and a person who is interested in dream analysis, I put a great amount of time and energy in attempting to pick apart my dreams. Also, my dreams can be quite revealing and prophetic, and this may be a gift from God. The important thing is not to be afraid of this gift.

After Yolanda's death, I discovered that my typewriter was missing from my office. I knew that she was going to take some paperwork home to type because it could not be done on the computer. I was puzzled because I could not find the typewriter, and finally Yolanda came to me in a dream and said, "It's in the back seat of the car." I looked in the back seat of both of my cars and found nothing. Later it was discovered that the typewriter was in the back seat of Yolanda's demolished car. The typewriter itself was also demolished. In another dream, Yolanda came to me and said, "Daddy, I have a lot more control over my life, now that I am no longer in Milwaukee." There are many interpretations to this dream, but I would rather not expound on any possible interpretation.

As my mind started to settle more, I found myself thinking more about Yolanda's autopsy. I was angry that the autopsy could be done by the medical examiner without the parent's consent. This made me wonder if this practice was money-driven rather than done for any legal or practical purpose. I also had to be persistent in trying to get a copy of the autopsy report. I called the medical examiner's office, and they finally released the report only after I identified myself as Dr. Earl Bracy. Everyone should be treated on an equal basis, but sometimes this doesn't happen in this country. Because I worked in surgery for twenty years of my life, I had no problems interpreting the autopsy report. I read it once and I have never read it again. My curiosity was satisfied, and I feel that anyone who finds themselves in this position should not only read the autopsy report but should also question the legality of performed autopsies without consent of the next of kin.

During Yolanda's funeral, I saw a lady videotaping the funeral, and I assumed that she was the mother of one of Yolanda's friends. I found out later that she was selling the videos. Sometimes people will also come to a funeral to see what they can find out. They don't always come with a pure heart.

I also believe that when we grieve, we become very primitive or primordial. By this, I mean, we can regress to a very infantile state. As I observed my son during the funeral, he and his first cousin were consoling each other. As I tried to console my son, I noticed that the two of them were speaking "gibberishly," and they were babbling to each other. One thing was for sure, even though they both are adults, I could not understand a word they were saying. Later, I wondered, was I babbling too, even though to myself I sounded coherent.

It is also interesting to point out that several of my white friends came to Yolanda's funeral, but only one white couple stayed for the entire service and none came to the grave site. One has to understand that sometimes people will come sign the book and show their respects and return back to their respective jobs. Some people are not good at funerals, and others don't care to look at the body. It's also interesting that once a person dies, the deceased person moves from being a person to a body. I'm sure one of Yolanda's comments to me if she was able to talk would have been, "See, Daddy, I told you so, they (white people) don't care about us, they won't even stay for the entire service." All Saints Catholic Church is in the heart of the inner city, and some people do have reservations about being in the inner city.

When Yolanda and Sonia were little girls, I always tried to reassure them that everyone was equal. Sonia never questioned me about it, but Yolanda was not buying it. Her comment to me was, "Well, if everybody's equal, then why do white people treat black people so bad?" I remember being speechless, and I don't remember if I gave her an answer to her question.

In conclusion, I would like to say that the way in which we're supposed to leave this world may be predestined. Also, if we look at the elements found in soil, we will find such things as sodium, potassium, calcium, nitrogen, and other elements that are also found in the human body. No one is less than anyone else, and when we die, these same elements return back to the earth and our souls move on. We all also breathe the same oxygen, and if that supply of oxygen is cut off, we all die.

When we grieve, it is important to feel the pain, go through the denial, shock, disbelief, numbness, anger, and finally acceptance and reaching a resolution. Losing my daughter in an automobile accident defines who I am, and there's nothing I can do about it other than accept it, learn from it, and teach others.

Six months after Yolanda's death, I remember flying to Alabama for my father's funeral. The flight out of Atlanta was quite turbulent, and for most of the flight, the plane shook excessively, and looking out the window at nothing but fierce-looking, thunderous clouds, it appeared that the plane was in a severe storm, and there was nothing the pilot could do but stay the course. Eventually, the pilot was able to ascend to a higher altitude above the cloud formation, and out of nowhere, the sun appeared and the sky was completely blue and peaceful.

When we experience a tragedy, it takes time to rise above the clouds and the turbulence and be able to enjoy the peaceful and tranquil blue skies.

As a practicing Catholic, since Yolanda's death, I also enrolled in a three and a half year lay ministry program (the Brother Booker Ashe Lay Ministry Program) and will complete this program in May of 2010. I am also a member of the choir (drummer), a Eucharistic minister, a lector, and for the last two years, I have participated in the secular Franciscan order meetings with my pastor, Father Carl Diederichs, and Brother Nicholas Schave. "Whereby our meeting is a time of prayer and sharing as followers of Jesus, exemplified by Saint Francis of Assisi. Franciscan brothers and sisters are dedicated to respecting all of creation, nurturing a life of peace, prayer, work, and joy, simplifying their material needs, and especially to showing compassion for and solidarity with the poor and the powerless." When change occurs in our lives, we are sometimes forced to change as well.

I spent many hours in solitude, writing and contemplating on the grounds of the Basilica of Holy Hill at Holy Hill, Wisconsin.

Holy Hill

I visited the fourteen Stations of the Cross at Holy Hill several times.

Simon helps Christ carry the cross.

Jesus falls while carrying the cross.

Depicts previous illustration

My daughter, the late Yolanda Bernadette Bracy

THE MAKING OF A BLACK PSYCHOLOGIST

In Loving Memory Of

Yolanda B. Bracy

Friday, August 5, 2005 / 12:00 noon

All Saints Catholic Church
4051 N. 25th Street / Milwaukee, Wisconsin

Reverend Carl E. Diederichs - Officiating

Arlene Skwierwaski - Keyboard
Willette Shaw - Cantor

Front cover of Yolanda's order of service

One of my favorite pastimes, drumming

CHAPTER EIGHT

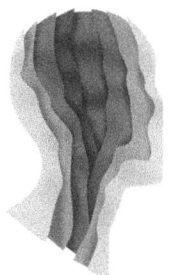

My Personal Grief (My Father's Death)

My father was a pastor and an assistant pastor of a Pentecostal church, which we attended as children. He served God faithfully for over seventy-five years of his life, and when he became ill, I became angry at God. I was thinking to myself that my father was saying, "My God, my God, why have you forsaken me?" As I processed my anger, I resigned myself to the fact that Jesus suffered on the cross and none of us will get through this life without suffering. My father lived to die, and his motto was, "We did not come here to stay." Even though he prepared us for this day, none of us was ready to let him go. When a family has not experienced a death, the circle has not been broken. When the circle is broken, it's easier to accept a death in the family, but broken or not, it's hard to let go of a parent or a child. It is extremely hard to watch a parent's health diminish. When I was a little boy, I used to walk behind my father because I could not keep up. I was starting to notice now that he was walking behind me because he couldn't keep up.

As I made more frequent trips to Alabama, I noticed that my father was becoming less lucid each time, and this troubled me considerably. Prior to starting radiation for prostate cancer, he spoke seriously to me about keeping some property in the family. He was over ninety years old when he told me this, and when he was ninety, he was still pushing the family lawn mower when the temperature was ninety degrees. I asked him if I could cut the grass, and he insisted on cutting it himself. He lived to be ninety-five years old, and he probably could have lived longer without radiation treatment for prostate cancer.

As his health declined, he became more confused and more bedridden. My mother asked him if he knew who I was and he said, "Sure, that's Earl." During this time, I was still angry at God, but when I looked into my father's face, I saw the face of God. There was a look of peace, contentment, love, compassion, and tranquility. The answer to the burning question of "why" was answered. I contemplated on the fourteen Stations of the Cross and what they meant, and I made a point to visit the Stations of the Cross at Holy Hill, Wisconsin, which is about fifteen minutes north of Milwaukee.

I also came to the realization that death is a part of life and life is a part of death. When our parents have lived out their lives, we still try to get more out of them when they may be ready to depart this life. We all have to remember that the seasons change and there's nothing we can do about it. We can water the grass and trees as much as we want, but at the end of the life cycle, grass turns brown, trees shed their leaves, and flowers die. At the end of life, we can pump in as much food, water, and medicine as possible, but the body dies. There is also the miracle of life and death. When we're born, we're born with a spirit or a soul and a unique personality or persona. When we were born our soul, spirit, persona, or personality came forth, and we presented as different and unique beings. I don't think we really die, but our spirit or soul goes forth to a different dimension.

In 2004, everybody gathered at the family home in Alabama, and Dad seemed more lucid. He knew all of his children, but he spent more time in his room, but his appetite seemed good. It is interesting to watch the aging process as it brings about a gradual decline.

During this visit home, I came to the realization that my father's condition would eventually decline more and we would have to let him go.

My father hung on for some time, and after having a visiting nurse come out, his condition worsened and he was moved to a hospice. My mother called me to let me know that his condition was weakening. I fluctuated between leaving for Alabama earlier in the week but decided to leave Friday the 13th, 2006.

The flight from Milwaukee was uneventful, but the flight from Atlanta to Mobile, Alabama, was turbulent and somewhat frightening. For some reason, it reminded me of the good and evil in the world. It had been a long time since I had had such a turbulent plane ride. Actually, the plane felt like it was going to go down any minute. My cell phone was in my briefcase, and as soon as we landed, I discovered that I had back-to-back calls from Alabama. My niece Lashawn was calling me to tell me that the minister had been summoned to the hospice and the family had gathered. When I got off the plane, I had to rent a car and the attendant went down the list of cars and I asked him to give me the first car that he named. At this point, I wasn't concerned about the type of rental car I was getting. I had to drive twenty miles from the airport to Daphne, Alabama.

When I arrived, I spoke into my father's ear to let him know that I was there. I held his hand and read John 14:1–4: "Do not let your hearts be troubled. You have faith in God; have faith also in me. In my father's house there are many mansions; if it were not so, I would have told you. I am going there to prepare a place for you and if I go and prepare a place for you, I will come back and take you to be with me that you may also be where I am."

He appeared to open his eyes, and a smile and a look of contentment came to his face. I felt that he was hanging on to my every word. Even though he was at end stage, his vitals were somewhat stable but he had a pulse rate of 124. He then started to experience some apnea, and he was starting to not respond to comments. Previously, he was in severe pain and pain medication was given in a suppository form.

My father always had a strong will, tenacity, determination, and his religious beliefs were stronger than any man I know. He was a hard worker, honest, and he found many innovative ways to take care of his family. I was now angry at God, not for taking him but for having him go through so much pain and agony. He was a man who fervently preached the gospel all of his life. The community loved him and his family loved him. He was also a pillar of strength, and he had gone through so much racism, oppression, and discrimination as a black man. He was born in the early 1900s in racist and segregated Alabama, and as his son, it hurt to know that he had been stripped of his dignity and manhood on many occasions.

My father had a white nurse whose name was Linda. Linda worked the third shift, and I saw her as an angel. She was kind, empathetic, and compassionate, and she explained things to the family. She explained the end stage process to us, and watching my father die reinforced the fact that the death process can be physically painful. Some family members were discussing my father's funeral, and I noticed some physical agitation coming from him. It is documented that hearing is the last thing to go, and family members should be careful what is discussed.

Nurse Linda informed the family that her daughter had died at the same hospice in the room across the hall about six months prior. She then became tearful, and as she did her work, she was humming songs most of the night and this must have been soothing to her. Our loved ones do not belong to us, and we all have to realize that at some point, we have to give them back. When the body shuts down, it's almost like you're reversing everything that was put into motion when we were a fetus. This is also akin to a beautiful plant that withers in the fall.

Although I was still angry at God at this point, I was constantly trying to make some sense out of pain and suffering and the meaning of life. The earth is billions of years old, and we only spend a few decades here. There has to be something beyond this life, and planet earth has to be a proving ground of sorts.

As I sat through the night with my father, it also occurred to me that my ex-wife's mother worked at the same place, taking care of white patients when I was in high school. At that time, black people were not accepted there as patients. It was most rewarding to me when I saw black nurses working there. Linda, the white nurse, was an angel to me because she afforded my father the dignity that he deserved, and she treated him like a total human being.

It is a difficult experience watching a loved one die, especially your own father. People have a tendency to ask how old a loved one was when they died. Many feel that because the person is old, it shouldn't matter but it does matter. Whether the person is twenty-six or ninety-six, the hurt is just as deep. When a person asks how old your loved one was, I think they're being very insensitive. As I sat with my father, I started to reflect, reminisce, and cherish the things that happened over the years. My father worked hard, and he believed in working us hard and keeping us busy. He would always say, "An idle mind is a devil's workshop." He didn't like us sleeping too much during the day, and another one of his expressions was, "Nothing comes to a sleeper but dreams."

As you reminisce, you wonder how time passed so rapidly. You think about your own mortality and what you would want people to do for you during the end stage. Death is the final stage of growth, and I wondered what it would be like when I am in my father's place. People sometimes want things done for their own convenience. I heard family members say things like, "I don't want him to die on Friday the 13th." Another concern was, "Will the suit match the casket?" My father died on January 14, and it was after everyone went home.

His funeral was a celebration and a home going, and even though he did not have the degrees that I do, he was a success and a blessing because he opened the door so that I, my siblings, his grandchildren, and his great grandchildren could walk through life with our heads erect.

In the mid-1980s, my father made a strong prediction. He said, "One day a black man and a white man will come together, and they're going to leave all of this garbage behind." I think he was referring to President Barack Obama and Vice President Joe Biden. This was a premonition he had that indeed came true.

St. Thomas Aquinas stated, "Every truth without exception—whoever may utter it—is from the Holy Spirit."

Upon reading my father's death certificate, I was appalled that the attending physician put "failure to thrive" on the death certificate. There was no mention of his prostate cancer, and I think that the correct cause of death is important for the present generation and for future generations. My father lived to be ninety-five, and about ninety-two of those years were good years. He impacted many lives in spite of being hampered by discrimination, oppression, and racism. He always had a smile on his face, and he spent much of his time encouraging others to smile. One of his many beliefs about life was, "We did not come here to stay."

My father and mother at his ninetieth birthday party

> **Happy 90th**
>
> Elder Gayle Bracy celebrated his 90th birthday with a dinner given in his honor at the Holiday Inn Express in Fairhope. His wife of 58 years, Maxine Bracy (pictured above with her husband), and their 11 children gave the dinner. A host of family and friends joined in the celebration.

Birthday announcement

My mother and father

Mercy Medical Hospice in Daphne, Alabama, where my father died

Last picture of my father enjoying good health

THE MAKING OF A BLACK PSYCHOLOGIST

Homegoing Celebration of
Elder Gayle Bracy

Sunrise	Sunset
February 15, 1910	January 14, 2006

Saturday, January 21, 2006
11:00 AM

Good Samaritan Sanctuary
7208 Twin Beech Road
Fairhope, Alabama

Elder Henry L. Crawford, Pastor

Front cover of my father's homegoing celebration service

Most of my father's grandchildren at the cemetery

Memorial Gardens Cemetery where my father is buried. At one time blacks could not be buried at this cemetery.

Family and friends

Headstone and grave site of my father, Elder Gayle Bracy

Gathering of family and friends

President Barack Obama and Vice President Joe Biden

CHAPTER NINE

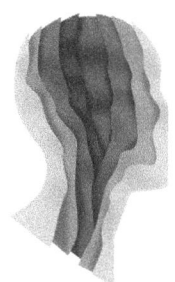

A Loving Mother

In 2008, we celebrated my mother's eighty-fifth birthday in a grand style, and many people in the community celebrated with us. I'm sure that she would say that the changes that took place in her eighty-five years were astounding. She was born musically inclined, and she still loves the piano and organ. My mother has always loved everyone, and her special smile can light up any room. Interestingly, all of her granddaughters and great granddaughters were blessed with her infectious smile. After my father died, my mother married another good man, Mr. Sandy Vachi Palmer, who also died, and she has since rebounded from his death.

My mother has also always had her favorite expressions. One of her expressions is, "There is a time and a place for everything." Whenever something was out of order, she would let it be known that she did not like it. If someone said something wrong at a wedding or a funeral or a church service, she would let it be known that she did not like it and it was out of place. It did not matter if it was the pastor, the copastor, the choir, or my father.

My mother was also born with common sense, and she always taught her children to use common sense in everything that we did. Having a mother and a father who were both spiritual and religious helped to bring a balance to my life and I'm sure to my siblings' lives.

Even as an adult, I talk to my mother about personal issues to get motherly advice, and a third eye perspective. It is also a given that if she tells you something, you can take it to the bank because she knows what she's talking about.

In 2007, I had a dream that I was asleep and in my bedroom with my pajamas on. In the dream, my mother walked in with her back bent even though she has always been quite healthy. She looked like she was my mother and my grandmother. As she came closer to me, she stated, "Get up, put your pants on, and straighten up," and when I did this, she said, "That's my boy." In real life I was a little down in the dumps, and in the dream, she was probably telling me not to give up and she was aware of my capabilities. When she was saying, "You're my boy," I think she was also saying, "I know you."

In speaking about God, my mother would always say, "He can make a way out of no way." She certainly found a way to do it. As children, we never went without having a good Christmas. All of us received the toys that we wanted, and we also received clothes, Christmas candy, and our own portions of fruit. My mother's food at Christmastime and at other times was the bomb. If she decided that she had a craving for a certain type of fish, she would pick me to walk to the fish store to purchase it. The distance to and from the store was about a mile, but that was nothing for me to walk, even in ninety-five-degree weather.

My mother's mother lived outside of Pensacola, Florida, in a town called Cantonment, and she would visit her mother frequently. She would almost always take one of her children with her, and I remember the excitement when it was my turn. The Greyhound bus ride from Fairhope to Mobile to Pensacola was extra special, even though we had to sit in the back of the bus.

We were definitely taught as children the way in which we should go, and it followed us into adulthood. When I came to Milwaukee as an eighteen-year-old, I always felt as if I had my mother on one side and my father on the other. Even if I did stray, it wasn't for very long because the teachings of both parents followed me.

My brother, Bishop Howard Bracy, and I both migrated to Milwaukee after high school and managed not to become either a victim or a perpetrator in any way, and I have to attribute a great deal of this to good parenting. We have to continue to teach our children that good seeds grow on good ground.

Whenever I go home, I still report to my mother. If I decide that I am going to drive to Biloxi, Pensacola, or Gulf Shores, Alabama, or wherever I decide to go, my mother is always informed. I do this out of a matter of respect, and even though I'm grown, I feel that it is the right thing to do. As a psychologist, I hear many adult children cursing their parents out and telling the parent to stay out of their m——f—— business. This is wrong and totally disrespectful, and eventually, one has to pay for their callous disregard and disrespect.

Being a psychologist, I have worked with many, many children who have never had their mothers in their lives, and I have no idea what it feels like to not have the presence of that maternal figure.

I truly appreciate the love, the guidance, and the nurturance that I received from my mother because without it, there would have been a deep void in my life and a deep wound that would have been extremely hard to heal. I continually tell myself that in achieving the success that I've achieved, I did not do it alone. It is true that behind every good man, there is a strong woman, and behind me stood my mother. Proverbs 6:20-23 says it all:

"Observe oh my son, the commandment of your father, and do not forsake the law of your mother. Tie them upon your heart, constantly bind them upon your throat. When you walk about, it will lead you, when you lie down, it will stand guard over you, and when you have awakened, it itself will make you its concern."

My mother's eighty-fifth birthday party

You are cordially invited
To attend an
85th Birthday Celebration
In honor of

Maxine Bracy Palmer

Friday, January 16, 2008
Holiday Inn Express
19751 South Greeno Road, Hwy 98
Fairhope, AL

Reception – 5:00p.m.
Dinner & Tribute – 6:00p.m.
Hosts: Children

My mother's birthday invitation

My mother playing the piano after her eighty-fifth birthday party

ABOUT THE AUTHOR

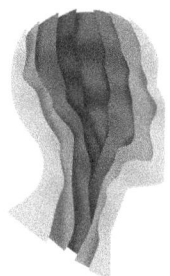

Dr. Earl Bracy candidly talks about his humble beginnings in the segregated South. He talks about his roots in Fairhope, Alabama, and how racial prejudice, injustice, discrimination, and racial stereotypes impacted his life and led him on a journey to improve the lives of others. He also shares his trials, tribulations, heartaches, challenges, obstacles, and joys. Many people do not fully understand the impact that discrimination and second-class citizenship have on a person's psyche. Dr. Bracy has lived through the era of "Jim Crowism" and is a witness to its negative effects. He shares many of his deepest feelings on many topics, including what it means to be a black male in America, a black Catholic, and a black clinical psychologist. He discusses the reaction that many people have to his three roles.

Dr. Bracy also worked as a cardiovascular perfusionist for fifteen years at hospitals in the Milwaukee area. He was also trained as a combat medic and surgical technician in the United States Army during the height of the Vietnam War.

For More Information

Dr. Bracy is available for lectures and seminars pertaining to stress management, race relations, interpersonal violence, and black-on-black violence. He talks a great deal about violence in his last book, entitled *Too Young to Die—Inner City Adolescent Homicides (A Psychological Autopsy)*.

For information on lectures and seminars, Dr. Bracy can be reached at Bracy Psychological Services and Stress Management Institute LLC, 5225 N Ironwood Rd., Suite 214, Glendale, WI 53217. Dr. Bracy can also be reached by calling 414-963-1115 or 414-379-8919.

E-mail address is Earl_Bracy@sbcglobal.net.

Milton Keynes UK
Ingram Content Group UK Ltd.
UKHW020621050324
438776UK00006B/1003